Praise for
A Culturally Proficient Response to the Common Core: Ensuring Equity Through Professional Learning

America's goal to reach proficiency for all students cannot be achieved without equity and a lens of social justice in the classrooms. *A Culturally Proficient Response to the Common Core: Ensuring Equity Through Professional Learning* gives not only theory and rationale for this important change in thinking, but also the guided steps to collaborate and reflect as part of the change process.

—**Carol Van Vooren EdD**
Assistant Professor
California State University, San Marcos
San Marcos, CA

I commend the authors for their courageous leadership as they address the need for teachers to connect students to learning with the addition of equity in the Common Core State Standards. Through this book teachers are called to action to self-reflect and to value cultural proficiency and advocacy as integral components of daily instruction and philosophy of inclusion. Applying the Inside-Out model, self-reflection, and the implementation of the Four Tools enhances learning, makes the learning relevant, and brings the student to education with an intentional investment in them and in their future as contributing members of a diverse society where all are valued.

—**Jan La Torre-Derby, EdD**
Retired Superintendent
Novato Unified School District
Novato, CA

The dynamic shift within the new school-community will task school leaders to approach CCSS through a Culturally Proficient lens in order to effectually reach the hearts and minds of the contemporary underserved student-community. This book, infused with CCSS, will challenge educators to *teach and lead* differently to close the learning gap, bring about greater equity in education, and increase the possibility for greater human capital for the next generation of students. CCSS with Cultural Proficiency will allow educators to look at this new paradigm shift not from a deficit model, but rather from an asset perspective.

—**Joseph M. Domingues**
Principal
Santa Maria High School
Santa Maria, CA

The authors have ensured that the use of Cultural Proficiency by educators supports the Common Core State Standards with the step toward that place where equity and access are realized for all learners. Equity and access, two of the pillars of cultural proficiency in education, are essential if meeting individual student needs is truly to occur.

—Kenneth Magdaleno, EdD
Associate Professor
California State University, Fresno
Fresno, CA

The authors continue to provide educators the cultural proficiency knowledge needed to meet the needs of all students regardless of the state or national standards! This book offers support of what those who are on the cultural proficient journey know; when they use the lens of Cultural Proficiency the outcome is better for all students. The message is clear, regardless of the initiative; cultural proficiency must be infused throughout the process!

—Thomas Christie
Multicultural School/Community Administrator
Lincoln Public Schools
Lincoln, NE

We need a lens for interpreting the Common Core State Standards in more equitable ways. The 5 Essential Elements for Cultural Proficiency does just that. As a result, the educational community can more clearly see how to create a classroom and school culture that is supportive and representative of each and every learner.

—Margo Gottlieb
Author and Teacher Educator
Illinois Resource Center and
World-Class Instructional Design & Assessment (WIDA)
Arlington Heights, IL

This book masterfully leads the reader from *thinking* about the Common Core through the lens of Cultural Proficiency to *planning*, and then *action*. The goal is clear, well supported with numerous case stories, and focused: access and opportunities to all students!

—Dr. Andrea Honigsfeld
Professor and Author
Molloy College
Rockville Centre, NY

This book provides a guidebook for teachers and leaders as we explore professional learning through the lens of Cultural Proficiency to ensure equitable approaches that close student access and achievement gaps. This resource text pushes, pulls, and nudges us into practice by providing action-planning templates for the reader's use. Using the concepts of Getting Centered and Going Deeper, the authors bring readers into case studies and provide a continuum from which you might assess your current levels and provide a pathway toward professional learning. A well-written and accessible text that will encourage interaction and taking the next step toward building a culturally proficient learning culture at your school or district.

—Jill Gildea, EdD
Superintendent of Schools
Fremont School District 79
Mundelein, IL

In this well-researched book about practice and science, the authors present relevant calls to action in terms of Cultural Proficiency as we public educators spend the next phase in our nation's growth helping students—ALL students—grow to the next level.

—Michael Lubelfeld, EdD
Superintendent of Schools
Deerfield Public Schools
Deerfield, IL

This book is an extremely rich and detailed resource for practitioners and leaders in the field of education. It avoids engaging in any of the political debate surrounding the Common Core Learning Standards and provides structures, frameworks, and specific strategies for schools to strengthen student outcomes with Cultural Proficiency as the lens. This work references important research and literature connections such that new practices are integrated and seamless as opposed to adding one more thing to the "plate."

—Lynn Macan, PhD
Superintendent
Cobleskill-Richmondville Central School District
Cobleskill, NY

A Culturally Proficient Response to the Common Core

A Culturally Proficient Response to the Common Core

Ensuring Equity Through Professional Learning

Delores B. Lindsey

Karen M. Kearney

Delia Estrada

Raymond D. Terrell

Randall B. Lindsey

Foreword by Gail L. Thompson

CORWIN

A SAGE Company

FOR INFORMATION:

Corwin

A SAGE Company

2455 Teller Road

Thousand Oaks, California 91320

(800) 233-9936

www.corwin.com

SAGE Publications Ltd.

1 Oliver's Yard

55 City Road

London EC1Y 1SP

United Kingdom

SAGE Publications India Pvt. Ltd.

B 1/I 1 Mohan Cooperative Industrial Area

Mathura Road, New Delhi 110 044

India

SAGE Publications Asia-Pacific Pte. Ltd.

3 Church Street

#10-04 Samsung Hub

Singapore 049483

Printed in the United States of America

A catalog record of this book is available from the Library of Congress.

ISBN 978-1-4833-1910-0

Acquisitions Editor: Dan Alpert

Associate Editor: Kimberly Greenberg

Editorial Assistant: Cesar Reyes

Production Editor: Amy Schroller

Copy Editor: Amy Rosenstein

Typesetter: C&M Digitals (P) Ltd.

Proofreader: Ellen Howard

Indexer: Jean Casalegno

Cover Designer: Gail Buschman

Marketing Manager: Stephanie Trkay

This book is printed on acid-free paper.

MIX
Paper from
responsible sources
FSC® C014174

14 15 16 17 18 10 9 8 7 6 5 4 3 2 1

Table of Contents

Foreword

In *A Culturally Proficient Response to the Common Core: Ensuring Equity Through Professional Learning*, Delores Lindsey and her co-authors use research, professional growth experiences, stories, and examples with the goal of helping school leaders use "Culturally Proficient practices" to not only successfully implement the new Common Core Standards, but more importantly to improve schooling outcomes for the students who have been historically underserved.

During the three decades that I've been an educator, I've become increasingly convinced that one of the main reasons why the US K–12 public school system has repeatedly failed to live up to its potential is the fact that most education reforms usually focus on *strategies* alone, instead of strategies *and* the crucial mindset work that must be done. In fact, since the publication of *A Nation at Risk*, the US K–12 public school system has been inundated with one education reform after another. However, to date, no reform has managed to solve the problems plaguing most urban, high-minority, and low-income schools. Consequently, the achievement gaps continue to exist, and African American, Latino, and low-income students continue to be disproportionately represented among the students who underachieve as measured by standardized test scores. These students are also more likely to be retained in a grade, suspended, expelled, and to drop out of school. Furthermore, teacher-training entities are still failing to adequately prepare prospective teachers and beginning teachers to work effectively with the students who have historically been underserved by the public school system.

The latest education reform is based on a Common Core Standards model. The underlying notion is that when states adopt a uniform set of standards to measure student progress, the public school system will improve. Nevertheless, Delores Lindsey and her co-authors were prescient enough to realize that unless the equity issue is added to the "mix," the latest reform venture will fail as dismally as previous education reforms have failed. In other words, these authors foresaw that the new *strategy* must also be coupled with the equity mindset work.

As Lindsey and her co-authors state, "For the Common Core to have impact, and for professional development to be effective, equity, access, and inclusion must be embedded into conceptions of Common Core. With these mindsets in place, educators will be well equipped to embrace and use all future reforms that emanate from government, the private sector, and our own professional efforts."

In short, individuals who are serious about school reform *and* equity will find a plethora of useful information in this timely, practical, informative, reader-friendly book.

Dr. Gail L. Thompson
Co-author of *Yes, You Can! Advice for Teachers Who Want a
Great Start and Great Finish With Their Students of Color*

Acknowledgments

We are mindful and are grateful for the many people who have contributed to the completion of this book: the patient support and sacrifices of family, the contributions of professional colleagues, and the inspiration of friends. Our words here are to honor their support for this work.

For me, Delores, co-writing this book has been another learning journey. I continue to learn about myself as an educator and grow as a writer. We knew this was the right time to write this book. As educators throughout the United States and Canada continue to plan for high-quality professional learning in support of teachers and leaders, we wanted to offer the lens of Cultural Proficiency as an approach for all students to achieve at high standards that prepare them for college and careers for the 21st century. I thank my co-authors for their expertise, their willingness to share their experiences, and their patience with me as a learner. I greatly appreciate and acknowledge the many educators with whom we work (the composite case stories) who continue to confront issues of inequity and injustice on behalf of students and employees. They, students and educators, are the people for whom we do this work. Thanks to Corwin's editors and staff for the professional and personal support you always give us. I give special thanks always to my husband, Randy, for being my co-writer and best friend.

For me, Karen, co-developing this book with my committed and experienced colleagues pulled and pushed my thinking out of its resting place and guided me to new learning and open-thought places. The chance to hear you talk about your work again was a reminder of the power of the cultural proficiency tools when used with your persistence and finesse. I also want to thank Jari for helping me better understand the long-term impact of teachers and coaches who practice culturally proficient or destructive behavior. Meshing academics and cultural proficiency together has promise for leading more students to better futures.

For me, Delia, working on this book has given me the opportunity to engage with truly wise individuals, who have guided me into truly fierce reflections on my daily interactions. They have taught me to appreciate the incredible importance of everyday practice. I am in awe on a daily basis of the teachers I work with, friends who support me, and the students we serve. These are brave individuals who have undertaken the task of building a new plane, even as we continue to fly it. Their resiliency and tenacity to meet these challenges head on, inspires me to delve more deeply into what I do and what I believe. It also reminds me I am a humble, but proud, servant of a world that can be. Thank you for your patience, and your time, as I find my way as a leader, a scholar, and a person.

For me, Raymond, the production of this book has allowed me to reach deep within myself and explore how the benefits of the Common Core might impact many underserved students. Educational reform that addresses basic curriculum, achievement outcomes and standards without giving equal importance to school/teacher/student interaction as an organic whole has always missed the boat. Using Cultural Proficiency as the partner lens when implementing the Common Core provides the tools to ensure that all diverse demographics are served in an equitable fashion. Most importantly, writing this book afforded me the opportunity to continue a cooperative 45-year equity journey with my best friend and colleague, Randy.

For me, Randy, it has been a growth experience to conceptualize and compose this book with colleagues who are also friends. When Raymond and I started this journey in 1970, I could not imagine working with Karen, Delia, and Delores on such an important project. This experience has been rewarding personally and professionally. Our collective work on issues and topics of social justice is now in its fourth decade, and this book provides the opportunity for us to use the print medium to apply current reform efforts in ways that meaningfully touch the lives of students who have been historically marginalized. To be able to write with Delores continues to be one of the joys of my life.

Our colleagues at Corwin have been and continue to support our work in deep, authentic ways. Dan Alpert, our acquisitions editor, continuously serves as "friend of the work of equity" and embodies the commitment to social justice we associate with Corwin. Appreciation goes to Cesar Reyes, Senior Editorial Assistant, whose high levels of support, responsiveness, and resourcefulness make the publication process proceed smoothly.

Publisher's Acknowledgments

Corwin gratefully acknowledges the contributions of the following reviewers:

Margo Gottlieb
Teacher Educator
Illinois Resource Center and World-Class Instructional
Design & Assessment (WIDA)
Arlington Heights, IL

Andrea Honigsfeld
Professor
Molloy College
Rockville Centre, NY

Jill Gildea
Superintendent of Schools
Fremont School District 79
Mundelein, IL

Michael Lubelfeld
Superintendent of Schools
Deerfield Public Schools—District 109
Deerfield, IL

Lynn Macan
Superintendent
Cobleskill-Richmondville Central School District
Cobleskill, NY

Zaretta Hammond
Education Consultant/Adjunct Instructor
Saint Mary's College, Kalmanovitz School of Education
Berkeley, CA

About the Authors

Delores B. Lindsey, PhD, a recently retired Associate Professor from California State University, San Marcos, has also served as a middle grades and high school teacher, assistant principal, principal, and county office administrator. Her primary focus is developing and supporting culturally proficient leaders. Using the lens of Cultural Proficiency, Delores helps educational leaders examine their organization's policies and practices, as well as their individual beliefs and values about cross-cultural communication. Her message to her audiences focuses on nurturing socially just educational practices, developing culturally proficient leadership practices, and using diversity as an asset and resource. Delores facilitates educators to develop their own inquiry and action research. She relies on the power of story and storytelling to enhance learning experiences. She asks reflective questions and encourages group members to use questions as prompts for their organizational stories. Her favorite reflective questions are: *Who are we?* and *Are we who we say we are?*

Karen M. Kearney, MA, is the Director of the Leadership Initiative and Senior Program Associate with the California Comprehensive Center at WestEd, a nonprofit research, development, and service agency that works with education and other communities to promote excellence, achieve equity, and improve learning for children, youth, and adults. For 10 years, her focus has been on transforming administrator and teacher preparation, professional development, and evaluation policies and programs so that educators are expected and supported to practice culturally proficient leadership. Prior to this, Karen was the state Executive Director of the California School Leadership Academy, a large state professional development and coaching network set on learning and practicing culturally proficient leadership. She served as a high school teacher, junior high vice principal, and led three different elementary and middle schools.

Delia Estrada is a PhD candidate at Claremont Graduate University and is currently principal at Taft Charter High School in Woodland Hills, California, with LAUSD. She has served as a middle school and high school teacher, program specialist for English language learners, history/social science specialist, and assistant principal. She concentrates her work on the fundamental belief that educators can and will meet the demands of eradicating inequity through collaboration, communication, and community building. She is committed to creating, using the tools of Cultural Proficiency, and building safe environments to engage in fierce conversation and reflective practice. In so doing, teachers will and are *capable* of influencing the world: one lesson and one interaction at a time. She also lives by the principle that laughter, relationship, and understanding make anything possible.

Raymond D. Terrell, EdD, is an Emeritus Professor, College of Education, Health, and Society, Miami University in Oxford, Ohio. He also served as a professor of Educational Administration and Dean of the School of Education at California State University, Los Angeles. He began his career as a public school teacher, principal, and assistant superintendent in the Princeton City School District in Ohio. He has more than 40 years of professional experience with diversity and equity issues in urban and suburban school districts. Ray lives in Cincinnati, Ohio, with his wife Eloise. They are both enjoying reading, writing, traveling, and spoiling adopted grandchildren.

Randall B. Lindsey, PhD, is Emeritus Professor, California State University, Los Angeles, and has a practice centered on educational consulting and issues related to equity and access. Prior to higher education faculty roles, Randy served as a junior and senior high school history teacher, a district office administrator for school desegregation, and executive director of a nonprofit corporation. All of Randy's experiences have been in working with diverse populations, and his area of study is the behavior of white people in multicultural settings. It is his belief and experience that too often members of dominant groups are observers of cross-cultural issues rather than personally involved with them. He works with colleagues to design and implement programs for and with schools and community-based organizations to provide access and achievement.

Randy and his wife and frequent co-author, Delores, are enjoying this phase of life as grandparents, as educators, and in support of just causes that extend the promises of democracy throughout society in authentic ways.

This book is dedicated to

*All educators who are making a personal commitment to learn and
practice culturally proficient values and behaviors to ensure students, especially those who have
been traditionally underserved, reap the benefits promised by the Common Core initiative.*

Introduction

We invite you to explore with us these and other critical questions posed in this book.

- *In what ways might the implementation of the Common Core State Standards (CCSS) differ from the ways teachers have been teaching and students have been learning for the past 15 years?*
- *What challenges are you and fellow educators confronting as you seek to fulfill the promise of the CCSS for all learners?*
- *What leverage opportunities might the CCSS provide educators as we structure and guarantee access to college and career readiness for historically marginalized and underserved students?*

THE INTENT OF THIS BOOK

At the writing of this book, school districts throughout 43 states and the District of Columbia are engaged in various stages of implementing the CCSS (some states are instituting similarly rigorous standards). Our intention in this book is to support your desire to ensure equity outcomes of CCSS by using the lens of Cultural Proficiency to examine and manage the professional learning that supports schools' and districts' implementation plans. We do not advocate for adding Cultural Proficiency as a new initiative or program. Rather, we propose that educators work collaboratively to integrate the Tools of Cultural Proficiency with their current work in serving the academic and social needs of students. Collaboration and integration focused on equity and access for all learners will be aimed at the CCSS for all students to achieve at levels higher than ever before. These higher levels of achievement mean that all students have access to curriculum materials and instructional strategies that will prepare them for college (entrance and exit) AND prepare them for their chosen workplaces and career paths.

A SHIFT IN THINKING: THE "SILVER LINING" OF NO CHILD LEFT BEHIND AND THE OPPORTUNITY OF CCSS

The concept and implementation of CCSS require a shift in thinking from the past 15 years, while preserving a significant achievement afforded by No Child Left Behind (NCLB). Whereas the mindset for the NCLB initiative was *satisfying high school exit criteria,* it also made our profession fully aware of the achievement gap. The use of disaggregated data is a significant opportunity provided by NCLB to be maintained as we move forward with CCSS. CCSS brings to us a focus on the thinking and performance skills necessary for *college and career readiness.* CCSS requires educators to think and plan broader than the minimum competencies mandated by NCLB. CCSS is a redesign and recalibration of the academic environment to provide access for higher order, critical thinking for all learners. In other words, CCSS can provide leverage for doing what we do best—teaching our students to think and perform.

FROM DESIGN TO DELIVERY— CONTINUOUS IMPROVEMENT

We invite and encourage you as educators to examine your beliefs, values, and assumptions about how students learn and what students need to learn to be college and career ready. Cultural Proficiency provides the equity lens for CCSS so that this new initiative stays focused on *college AND career* readiness rather than risk becoming *college OR career readiness.* In Chapter 12, we offer you and your colleagues the opportunity to develop your Culturally Proficient Professional Learning Action Plan as a systematic way to support implementation of the CCSS in your school and classroom. Professional learning supports implementation planning from the design stage using new or alternative curriculum to the delivery of that curriculum content (i.e., instructional strategies) and assessment of student progress for improvement of instruction. Figure 1 illustrates the interdependent relationship of quality professional learning delivered through the lens of Cultural Proficiency. The result of this design is a clearly stated plan focused on clearly stated student outcomes that embrace the diversity of learners in our schools.

As noted in Figure 1, teachers and administrators who work collaboratively to identify their quality professional learning standards can guide their Culturally Proficient Professional Learning Action Plan (CPPLAP) from the early design stage to the implementation stage using

Figure 1 Interdependent Relationship of Quality Professional Learning Delivered Through a Cultural Proficiency Lens

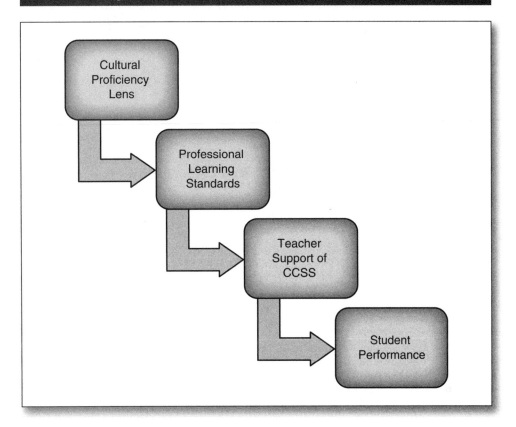

the continuous improvement process. Student assessment data examined through the lens of Cultural Proficiency allows for continuous monitoring of the CPPLAP's outcomes and goals. A prominent feature of this continuous process is benchmarking the formative assessments through the lens of Cultural Proficiency and thereby providing an equitable learning environment.

CULTURAL PROFICIENCY AND PROFESSIONAL LEARNING

This book integrates the *Tools of Cultural Proficiency* with quality *Standards for Professional Learning* as one approach to examining and implementing the Common Core State Standards. The authors believe the language, the tools, and the practices of Cultural Proficiency are missing from the current conversations and implementations of Common Core plans. We also believe that topics of equity and access to curriculum and quality instruction for histori-cally marginalized and underserved groups of students have been largely absent from professional development/learning programs for the past 15 years. Those of you who are familiar with the Cultural Proficiency books will recognize the definitions and descriptions of the Four Tools of Cultural Proficiency in Chapter 3. If you are new to the conceptual framework, you will find Chapter 3's description of the Tools of Cultural Proficiency to be helpful without needing to read other books in the series first. Each Cultural Proficiency book is an application of the Tools to a particular setting. This book integrates quality professional learning standards with the Tools of Cultural Proficiency for teams of educators to execute schoolwide and dis-trictwide implementation plans of CCSS to support all learners.

Resources Section

The resources section of the book provides useful tools to enhance ongoing learning, a matrix of how to use other Cultural Proficiency titles, and a Book Study Guide:

- The Book Study Guide is intended for use in deepening individual understanding of the content and for use in collegial professional learning.
- The matrix lists other Cultural Proficiency books and the essen-tial questions that guided the books' development. The guiding questions are intended to promote your deeper learning and your professional growth as well.

As you will see in the matrix, 15 books on Cultural Proficiency are now available or in production. Each of the Cultural Proficiency titles has a distinct application of the Tools of Cultural Proficiency, and the matrix is organized to inform you of which book(s) may be appropriate for your use. Figure 2, The "Apps" of Cultural Proficiency, is a pictorial representa-tion of the Cultural Proficiency books. The original and core book, *Cultural Proficiency: A Manual for School Leaders,* now in its third edition, presents our most detailed description of the Tools of Cultural Proficiency. The books radiating from the "Manual" also present the basic "Tools" in an applied manner relating to the books' intent (e.g., instruction, coaching, etc.)

A FORESHADOWING OF WHAT'S AHEAD

Chapter 1 introduces you to the purpose of the book and to important terms and the way we use them in the context of this book. Chapter 2 provides

Figure 2 The "Apps" of Cultural Proficiency

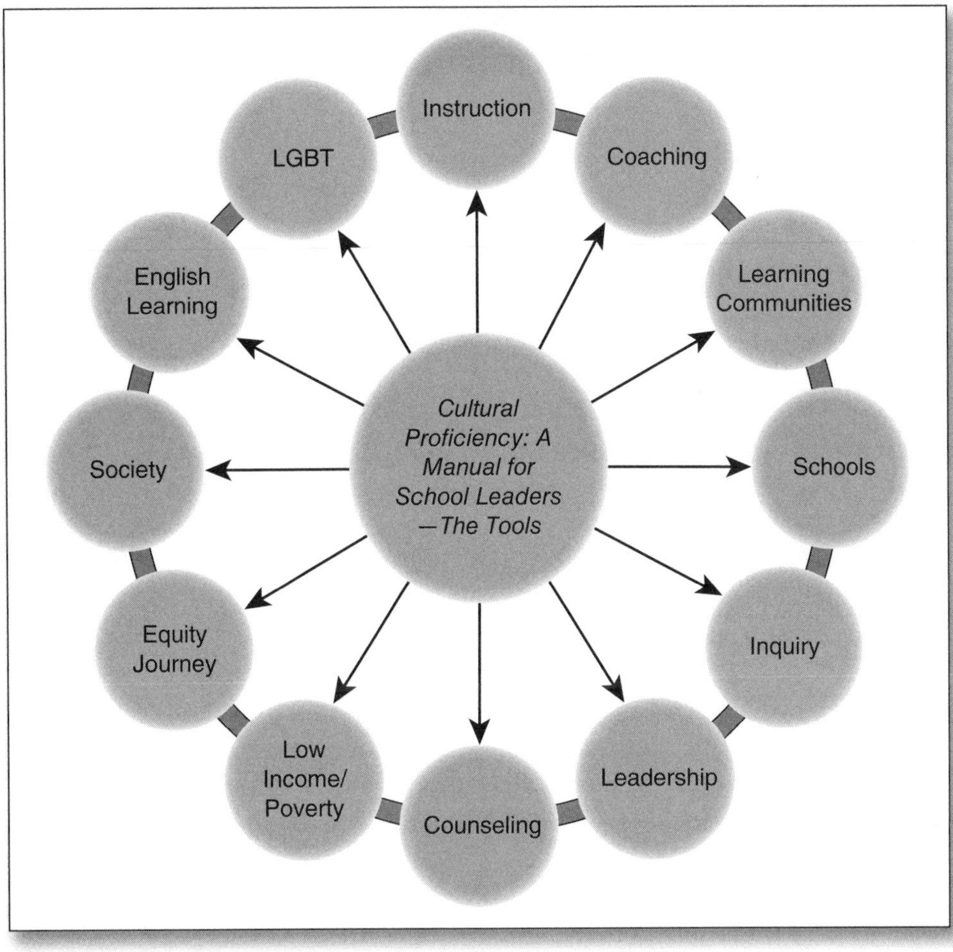

a historical and contextual background for school change and initiatives. You will see clearly why we are at this important juncture for US education. Chapter 3 presents descriptions and definitions of the Four Tools of Cultural Proficiency. Chapters 4, 5, and 6 provide the context for the promise, the opportunities, and challenges of implementing CCSS.

Chapters 7–11 capture the work of school leaders as they use the lens of equity to implement the CCSS. The stories in these five chapters are composites of actual school leaders, teachers, staff members, districts administrators, and parents with whom we have worked over the past two years as they prepared and implemented early stages of CCSS using Cultural Proficiency. Each chapter is framed using one of the 5 Essential Elements of Cultural Proficiency integrated with one of the standards of professional learning. As you read these five chapters, remember that these elements and standards do not stand alone; rather, they function interdependently and holistically as standards for behaviors and desired actions. For the purposes of illustration and explanation, we offer them one chapter at a time with case stories to show the impact and influence of the elements combined with the standards.

Chapter 12 is the "Now What" chapter. *Now that you know what you know, to what are you willing to commit?* We provide you with an Action Plan template for implementation of your CPPLAP. Your Action Plan is grounded in the conceptual framework of Cultural Proficiency and quality Professional Learning Standards. The Action Plan establishes clear outcomes and goals that are consistent with the Common Core Standards of preparing all students for college and career options by the end of high school graduation.

YOU AND WE

We use the pronoun "you" to personalize our relationship to the reader of this book. The pronoun "we" refers to the co-authors of the book. We have combined our years of work as educators, school administrators, and scholar practitioners to bring you our experiences, our research, and our best thinking about the importance of responding to and implementing and sustaining the Common Core Standards in ways that provide all students access to college and career opportunities unlike anytime in this nation's history.

THE FORMAT OF THIS BOOK

This book is designed as an individual guide for reflection and action. It is also designed to be used with colleagues in small groups or in large groups as a book study or a guide for developing a school or district CPPLAP for implementation of the Common Core. Each chapter has lined spaces for you to write your individual reflections to questions integrated with the text and suggestions for reflection and action at the end of each chapter. The reflections and the dialogues with your fellow learners will enhance your learning. And your learning community will be enhanced by diversity of perspectives, experiences, and expertise. We wish you well and join you on your lifelong journey of becoming culturally proficient.

Part I

Commitment to Equity, Transformative Change, and Implementation

The goals of equitable education outcomes and the Common Core State Standards (CCSS) can be mutually supportive if approached as being inclusive and interdependent. Educational and school reforms are historical processes that have shaped, molded, and buffeted schools for well over a century. Similarly, ensuring equitable access and academic outcomes has a long, often-tortuous history in the United States and Canada.

A virtue of No Child Left Behind is that it made achievement gaps public. There is no going back. Educational inequity has been uncovered and made part of the national educational discourse. Though flight from low-performing school districts to enclaves of historically advantaged communities continues, excuses for marginalizing historically underserved students and their communities are being eroded. It is into this mix the CCSS can drive changes in instruction, curriculum alignment, and assessment in ways that focus educators' attention on equitable access to higher order learning and, thereby, ensure equitable educational opportunities and outcomes for students in ways not yet seen.

Part I contains the Introduction and six chapters, each of which is a building block to understanding equity and reform in ways that will empower you to consider the changes you will want to make in your educational practice and the way you will want to lead in your school or district. These six chapters present information designed to deepen your learning and, also, opportunities for personal reflection and dialogic opportunities to explore professional learning occasions with colleagues. Upon completion of these chapters, you will be well equipped to delve into Part II and learn how to use the 5 Essential Elements as standards to guide your individual educational practice and to lead professional learning experiences with colleagues.

Chapter 1 is designed to guide you in examining the mindsets you and your colleagues hold for important concepts such as reform experienced as transformative change and equitable opportunity promising higher learning opportunities and outcomes for all students. Chapter 1 also supplies definitions of key terms used throughout the book. A central thesis that winds through this book, and all other Cultural Proficiency books that we have constructed, is the power of assumptions, both those held by individual educators and those that become ingrained in our school's policies and practices. It is our mindsets, or sets of assumptions, about equity and change as embodied in the CCSS that can shape successes with our students.

Chapter 2 provides you with important information that will help inform and shape your perspective on your role as an educator. The winding history of school reform and initiatives for educational equity are presented and discussed as social forces that when understood, can help form our views of the tasks that lie before us. Knowing that the achievement gap has always been with us and is now part of ongoing discussions in schools and the general public is an important perspective. Similarly, having knowledge of the slow pace of educational equity is another important perspective. Then, when these two perspectives are brought together, they equip with you with what Fullan (2003) calls a moral imperative for closing access and achievement gaps.

Equipped with knowledge of mindsets, reform as transformative change, and issues of equity, you are now prepared to make expert use of Chapter 3. This chapter presents a detailed explanation and illustrations of the Tools of Cultural Proficiency. You will read and learn about how the Barriers to Cultural Proficiency serve to limit and deny equity, the Guiding Principles as core values to overcome the Barriers, the Continuum as a range of unhealthy to healthy behavior and practices, and the Essential Elements as standards for behavior and practices that are derived from the Guiding Principles. When taken together, these four tools are powerful instruments for you and your colleagues to use in guiding powerful learning opportunities for yourselves and your students.

Chapter 4 provides an overview of the promise and main features of the CCSS. Particular attention is paid to the shifts in teaching and learning that accompany successful implementation of CCSS.

Chapter 5 pays in-depth attention to leadership requirements for the successful implementation of CCSS. Once you have completed this chapter, you will be well informed in how to lead equitable, transformative change efforts in your school.

Chapter 6 uses the unorthodox word "stuckness" in the title. Through the experiences of one principal, we crafted this chapter to describe how using the Guiding Principles of Cultural Proficiency can jump-start the journey to transformative change. Collective efficacy and academic optimism inform the beliefs that our students can learn and that we can teach them.

1

Common Core and Cultural Proficiency

A Commitment Toward Equity

Equity is the fundamental value, visible through public commitments and specific practices. Supporting values—continuous learning for all, collaboration, and collective responsibility for everyone learning—further enliven equity at each school. These values together are non-negotiable drivers of improvement.

—Gleason & Gerzon, 2013, p. 120

GETTING CENTERED

The epigraph is from Gleason and Gerzon's research study of four Title I case schools to identify common themes for all students achieving at high performance levels. The researchers found that educators at these four schools *lived* their values that supported equitable learning for their students. Their values were not only their *espoused* values but also their ways of being, ways of teaching, and ways of learning. Take a moment and reread Gleason and Gerzon's quote. Now, think about the espoused values at your school, usually found in your school's vision and mission statement or list of core values. In what ways do these values become *lived* values and actions? What evidence and artifacts would you use to demonstrate to visitors your lived values? In what ways do the current espoused values prepare you and your colleagues for implementing and sustaining the Common Core State Standards (CCSS)? What might be missing from your school's stated values? Please use the space below to record your feelings, your questions, and your thinking as you consider these questions.

WHY THIS BOOK?

We assume that you selected this book because of your commitment to equitable outcomes for all students. Like us, you are keenly aware that though the United States has made progress in narrowing access and achievement gaps in recent years, you might wonder how the CCSS will influence your ability to provide for students' needs. You are also aware that though the CCSS implies equity through use of phrases such as "all students," our reality is that equity can never be assumed—it must be explicitly expressed. This book responds to the urgency to fulfill the promise of the CCSS for all students, with a decided emphasis on "all." Given the richness and complexity of the diversity in today's schools, educators must be well prepared to ensure the CCSS involves a shift in teaching and learning that better prepares all students to be ready for college and the workplace when they graduate from high school.

This book is not about a blame game. This book is about understanding one's own mindsets and those of our colleagues to help us create even better educational experiences for our students. The journey to understanding equity and inequity begins with the individual. The journey begins with you and with me and with us. This chapter begins a carefully crafted journey in developing Culturally Proficient Professional Learning. This chapter guides you in reflecting on the manner in which your assumptions and mindsets help determine your values and beliefs for being successful in working with diverse communities. Enjoy the journey as it informs and empowers your continued success as an educator.

MINDSETS ARE WHO WE ARE

Cultural Proficiency is a mindset we use to view and experience the world around us. If our environment constitutes only people who are culturally like us, we may develop a mindset that literally cannot witness the experiences of others, no matter whether other cultural groups are having positive or negative experiences. The danger of limited exposure to others is that we may develop assumptions and beliefs informed by our lack of experiences that lead to stereotyping people who are different from us. Cultural Proficiency is about opening ourselves and our school or district to acknowledge the experiences of those not being successful in our schools. We are able to recognize the barriers our students face and, for us as educators, to be able to use our students' cultures as assets on which to build educational programs.

In our work over the past 20 years, we have used many analogies to communicate that Cultural Proficiency is a process, not a thing or an event. Some of the more prevalent analogies are:

- Cultural Proficiency as a mindset,
- Cultural Proficiency as a worldview,
- Cultural Proficiency as perspective,
- Cultural Proficiency as a mental model,
- Cultural Proficiency as a journey, and
- Cultural Proficiency as a lens through which to view and experience the world.

Pick the analogy that works for you. This book is about and for you. We have designed the book for use in your personal and professional development and for teams of educators devoted to educating students from all cultural groups in our communities and schools.

The journey of Cultural Proficiency involves recognizing the beliefs that create mindsets. Beliefs that relate to race, ethnicity, gender, social class, religion, ableness, or sexual orientation block effectiveness in cross-cultural communications and problem solving. It usually takes an awakening experience to challenge uninformed, negative cultural beliefs and their underlying assumptions. The personal story that follows is intended as an illustration provided by a colleague and his path to self-discovery.

Two of our authors have worked with the Oxnard California Police Department over the past several years. We supported the members of the department learning how to use the Tools of Cultural Proficiency and to adapt the tools to their law enforcement practice. That setting provides an apt description of the power of mindset. After several sessions, Eric

Sonstegard, Special Operations Division Commander, shared his experience of a changed mindset as he became increasingly aware of diversities and inequities that exist in society:

> *I wanted to share something with both of you that I'm not sure I can articulate accurately in an e-mail but I'll try my best. J.*
>
> *I know both of you are partially aware of my background and the fact that I grew up in a predominately white, upper-class neighborhood and attended a Lutheran University. Looking back, before I met both of you, I lived my life with what I characterize as "blinders" on. I was relatively successful in everything I did and had absolutely no idea about the advantages I had in life. Even as I progressed through my law enforcement career, I was woefully unaware of my place in society and the different cultures that surrounded me each day. It is very easy to do this when you work with police officers like yourself all day and then go home to a neighborhood that is very homogenous in its demographics. Since I met both of you and started on this journey with our cultural proficiency curriculum, I feel like some type of "code" was unlocked inside of me and I view everything around me different. By everything. . . , I mean everything. I can't read a newspaper article, watch the evening news, listen to the radio, or talk with friends without relating it to issues we've emphasized over the past few years. The analogy I like to make is if you've ever seen the movie* The Matrix. *They go through the movie viewing everything around them as it is, but at the end of the movie, Keanu Reeves's character is able to see all of the inner-workings behind everything around him. I feel like I can finally see through the superficiality of many things around me.*
>
> *I know that's a lot to digest, but there are very few people that understand or I can talk about it with. I guess I just want to thank you for being who you guys are and I'm blessed, both personally and for the department, that I met you. My one disappointment is that it took me 39 years to finally figure some of these things out. JJ.*

"Blinders" and "code" are weighty concepts. However, at this point you might ask, quite appropriately, "Though this is interesting, what does it have to do with educational reform?" Our response is, there are several concepts in this book to challenge or inform your beliefs and mindset about educational reform as well to inform you about marginalized groups' consistent struggles for equitable access and outcomes throughout our history. Officer Sonstegard gave us permission to share his mindset breakthrough in the expectation that reading of the personal experience of someone outside of education would serve as a useful illustration uncluttered by our education experiences.

REFLECTION

Take a few moments and think about the passages above. What comes to mind for you? What are your reactions? What new questions are surfacing about who you are? What new questions are surfacing about your school or district? Please use the spaces below to record your thinking.

_____

_____

_____

_____

This chapter describes the shift that must occur in teaching and learning by confronting beliefs, values, and deeply held assumptions about teaching and learning that have stymied educators' efforts to narrow and close access and achievement gaps. Each subsequent chapter provides a carefully crafted sequence of information and activities designed to guide you in becoming the educator you want to be and your school in becomimg a school that serves all students in an equitable manner.

The CCSS initiative is the current attempt to reform the American educational system. For the past 50 years, US public education has proposed to operate with a philosophy that it will serve as the foundation for providing the citizenry with tools that can help to sustain a democracy. At least three prominent and competing perspectives are present regarding CCSS:

- Some proponents of education reform hold that the promises of school reforms to date have been unrealized and this newest iteration of reform is embraced as the panacea to produce positive learning outcomes that lead to students' college and career readiness.
- Others view CCSS as just another step along a path to nowhere for many historically underserved students.
- Still a third group is wary of CCSS as an attempt to undermine local control and to nationalize curriculum.

In this book, we don't attempt to confront those different perspectives, only to acknowledge their existence and to make a case that whatever drives change initiatives must be tailored to the needs of all students. Therefore, we use CCSS as the frame for meeting the needs of all students and for writing this book. The book is designed in ways that can be applied to the various state-level modifications of CCSS.

The purpose of this book is to guide Culturally Proficient Leaders, including teachers, counselors, and administrators, as you:

- Bring an equity focus to the CCSS without losing the gains/progress from using No Child Left Behind's approach to disaggregating data for closing/narrowing access and achievement gaps;
- Embed the lens of Cultural Proficiency in the phrase "teach and lead differently" inherent in the CCSS;
- Ensure rigor, meaningful curricula and assessment, and higher order thinking for all students;
- Demonstrate how Cultural Proficiency is the lens for school leaders to create conditions that make the Common Core accessible for all students;
- Ensure the Common Core be possible and achievable for historically underserved students; and
- Deepen and extend educators' learning and experiences as they continue to become true professional learning communities.

THE GOOD, THE BAD, AND THE UGLY OF THE CCSS

In this book, we explore the potential good, bad, and ugly of the CCSS approach. Questions that guide us are: Will the CCSS produce positive academic outcomes for students? More importantly, will the CCSS produce positive outcomes for *all* students in a way that is different from past and current practices that continue to result in major gaps and disparities between and among different demographic groups of students? What is there in this prescribed set of standards and accountability markers that projects success? In what ways might the Common Core offer educators an opportunity to push the reset button and develop unique ways of delivering education and producing different outcomes?

These and other questions are yet unanswered and are useful to guide our work. To those questions we propose a new set of questions relevant to implementation of the CCSS and the education of all of our students:

- In what ways might we maintain a focus for the disproportionate assignment of African American, Latino, and Aboriginal First Nations students to classes for students with exceptionalities?
- In what ways do we maintain a focus for the disproportionally higher rates of suspensions, expulsions, and other sources of discipline that relegate inordinate numbers of African American, Latino, and Aboriginal First Nations students to be excluded from learning opportunities?

These are the kinds of questions that the lens of Cultural Proficiency helps us address in this book.

COMMON CORE SUPPORTS EDUCATORS AND STUDENTS TO BE CO-LEARNERS

Elementary schools have had a common core from their earliest beginnings. A set of common, *agreed-upon* standards that led to an *agreed-upon* curriculum was necessary to teach reading fundamentals to all students. Yet we know that the major failure or the defining factor in the outcome gaps has been the inability to provide all students with equitable resources to reach this reading baseline on which other learning is built.

School curricula are seemingly simple, yet as educators we know of their levels of complexity. Curriculum theorists (Banks, 2006; Delpit, 1995; Meier, 2002) have long referenced formal curriculum as those things taught intentionally in classrooms. These theorists also recognize that curriculum emanates from two seemingly unrelated sources. On the one hand, content for the formal curriculum is usually dictated by a combination of input from local, district, and state educational sources. To those sources, CCSS now provides a nationally approved set of standards. In addition to these formal sources, a powerful, real-life curriculum is lived out daily in classrooms, homes and in the communities of students that plays a major role in academic outcomes (Smith, 1996/2000). These realities, in fact, tend not to be very common across students' backgrounds and cultures, nor are they common across the backgrounds and cultures of the various teachers who will be the learning facilitators for these students.

In actuality, the cultures of those of us who are educators are often very different from the students in our classes. The choice is ours. We can let these cultural differences be an insurmountable problem. Or the culturally diverse classrooms can serve as rich laboratories that contribute to the growth and development of educators and students alike. The latter choice resonates in this book.

FROM REFORMING TO TRANSFORMING

Many previous educational reforms seemed to have had great potential for providing success for all; however, they often failed in rapid implementation processes that ignored or were oblivious to the cultures of the students. This invisibility of the power of culture has been exacerbated over the past 15 years by myriad forces—budget cutbacks and a lack of resources to support appropriate class size; inadequate instructional materials; demands from federal and state mandates for required, high-stakes standardized assessments; closing underserved schools; opening competing private/charter schools; rewards and sanctions related to testing; limiting educators' professional learning resources to mandated programs; and replacing principals and teachers based on schoolwide test scores. Often, some of the forces were presented as silver-bullet education reforms. The failure of many of these reforms is situated in what Hargreaves and Fullan (2012) refer to as the *five fallacies of misdirected education change:*

Excessive speed,

Standardization,

Substitution of bad people with good ones,

Overreliance on a narrow range of performance metrics, and

Win-lose inter-school competition. (p. 41)

So, rather than re-forming or trying to reshape schools, today's culturally proficient leaders are moving toward transformative actions. Shields (2010) describes three types of leadership, as a progression of ever-deepening change processes:

- Transactional leadership involves a reciprocal interaction in which the intention is for agreement and both parties benefit from the decision. For example, decisions in which faculty and principal agree to twice-monthly meetings that focus on improving literacy skills for all students are transactional leadership behaviors.
- Transformational leadership focuses on improving organizational effectiveness. Continuing with the example of improving student literacy, faculty agrees with principals to engage in professional development for instructional improvement that focuses on literacy literature and skill development.
- Transformative leadership recognizes that gaps in student literacy are found in inequities that are generational and correlated with students' demographic groupings. Continuing with the literacy examples, faculty and principals collaboratively challenge practices that marginalize students and press for equitable academic access and outcomes.

As you proceed through the book, you will see evidence of Hargreaves and Fullan's cautions as well as Shields' typology of leadership. Cultural proficiency is not a competitive quick fix but rather an intentional examination of self and our organizations in order to develop core values that honor and educate all students. Culturally proficient leadership, likewise, integrates Shields' descriptions of leadership into a seamless approach that recognizes day-to-day realities of school management alongside future-focused, systemic, transformative change in how students are served.

ASSUMPTIONS OF THIS BOOK

The coauthors held the following assumptions as we prepared this book:

- The CCSS were adopted by states as a way to improve education opportunities for all learners.
- The CCSS were prepared through a collaborative effort to ensure students across the United States would have access to an agreed-upon "core" of standards to help prepare them to enter college and the workplace upon graduating from high school.
- Students learn best when they are in schools and classrooms of teachers and administrators who demonstrate a value for their cultures and their families.
- Educators are the most important resource for student achievement during the school day.
- Educators working effectively with students' parents and guardians are important resources for supporting student achievement beyond the school day.
- Educator growth and development is an intentional, continuous process supported by systemwide, high-quality, professional learning and development.
- Professional learning viewed through the lens of Cultural Proficiency ensures equitable approaches to closing the student access and achievement gaps.

DEFINITION OF TERMS

The following terms are defined as they are used to support you as you read this book:

Culturally Proficient learning and leading is distinguished from other diversity and equity approaches in that it is anchored in the belief that a person must clearly understand one's own assumptions, beliefs, and values about people and cultures different from one's self to be effective in cross-cultural settings.

Access is the opportunity for preK–12 students to fully participate in high-level curricular and instruction programs of the school.

Common Core (Standards) is the most recent effort of educators and policymakers to identify and organize what our American students should know and be able to do by Grade 12 to graduate immediately ready for success in college and careers.

CCSS is the acronym for Common Core State Standards, often shortened to Common Core.

Equity is fairness and justice in assessing and providing for student academic and social needs.

College and Career Readiness is ensuring that students graduate high school ready to enter college and pursue a career.

Communities of Practice (Professional Learning Communities, Learning Communities) are formal and nonformal settings for educators to reflect on practice and to engage in professional learning.

Student Success/Achievement is meeting annual performance measures that ensure successful high school graduation.

THEORY OF ACTION FOR THIS BOOK

As authors, we offer teachers and school leaders a theory of action that will afford you an opportunity to enrich and enhance yourselves as implementers and facilitators of the Common Core, thus increasing success possibilities for all students. We offer the Tools for Culturally Proficient practices as an equity lens to examine the implementation process for the CCSS in your districts and schools.

Culturally Proficient educators use mindfulness, intentionality, reflection, and dialogue as baseline practices for connecting educators' beliefs, values, and culture with the beliefs, values, and culture of the students and the communities in which they serve. We invite you to join us on this journey of applying theory into the daily practice of engaging with your school community. This theory of action allows school leaders to add the fourth "R" to reading, 'riting, and 'rithmetic to include *relationships*.

This book presents the Four Tools of Cultural Proficiency as the foundation for addressing the continuing need to narrow and close access, achievement, and educational gaps in the United States and Canada. Although the conversation about a universal curriculum has been around for almost 30 years, only recently has the United States focused on a set of common standards from which to develop curriculum and assessments for K–12 education. Our question is, *In what ways do the CCSS help or challenge us in addressing equity and diversity?* Although the CCSS do not necessarily confront inequity directly, the outcomes of college and career readiness for all students are certainly implied. As we implement practices and learning required to meet the expectations inherent in the CCSS, we have opportunities to better address equity issues through culturally proficient actions and policies. Devising culturally proficient actions entails confronting barriers to reform initiatives such as the CCSS that exist within ourselves and our schools and districts as we continue to improve our craft and profession.

This book is composed of reflective and professional learning dialogic activities to guide you and your colleagues to do the one thing you want to do most, which is to support each and every student to be successful. The Tools of Cultural Proficiency guide you to understand your own assumptions about the students you serve, to know your values relative to equity issues, to create change within your practice, and to create teaching and learning environments that are relevant and rigorous for all learners. The book contains an *Implementation Rubric* to help leaders develop culturally proficient responses to the Common Core. Chapters 6 through 10 employ a blend of case stories and personal disclosure experiences to illustrate and demonstrate reflection and dialogue. The five chapters are shaped around the 5 Essential Elements as the Action Plan for Culturally Proficient Professional Learning unfolds for Lupe, the principal of a local middle school who faces the challenges and success of implementing the CCSS.

GOING DEEPER

Before you read any further, what are your thoughts about this opening chapter? In what ways do you expect this book to meet your learning needs? In what ways has this first chapter supported your knowledge and needs about teaching, learning, and leading the CCSS? What new questions do you now have? Please use the space below to record your thinking.

DIALOGIC ACTIVITY

With a group of your colleagues, engage in a dialogue to reach shared understanding of *a school culture in support of all learners performing at levels higher than ever before.* Continue the dialogue throughout small learning communities in your school district. Once shared understanding has been reached, what might be some resources, strategies, and structures that could be developed and activated to support all learners, with emphasis on achieving college *and* career readiness?

Chapter 2 begins our exploration of why an equity-based approach to the Common Core is needed. School reform is not new and, in fact, is part of a decades-long commitment to continuous improvement. However, only in the last few years have reform efforts begun to address persistent, historical inequities that are now well documented as access and achievement gaps. The information is this chapter will provide a rich context as you proceed to ensure that all of our students have access to high-quality education outcomes.

2 History and Hope for Changing Schools

Education law and policy reforms and their implementation occur in overlapping loops through a sort of evolutionary, historical process.

—Benjamin Michael Superfine, 2013, pp. 35–36

GETTING CENTERED

When you use the terms *reform, educational reform,* or *transform,* what comes to mind? When you hear colleagues use the terms *reform, educational reform,* or *transform,* what comes to mind? Take a few moments and reflect on how those terms are used by you, by your colleagues, and by the larger communities we serve. Use the space below to record your recollections of how the terms are used—context, focus, judgment, and so on.

_____

_____

_____

_____

    The purpose of this chapter is to provide you with a context for experiencing the Common Core State Standards (CCSS) and any subsequent reform that you may encounter during your career. Essential to understanding Culturally Proficient Professional Learning is knowing that commitment to all students learning at high levels has been a slow, evolving process. Understanding the history and context of educational reform and change equips you for making informed decisions about your ongoing professional development as well as guiding the professional development of your school and school district. When you have completed this chapter, you should be able to:

- Articulate an understanding of how mindsets shape perception.
- Make summary comments on the evolution of educational reform in the United States.
- Describe the ways in which educational reform and continuous improvement for transformative change inclusive of all demographic groups of students may be similar in definition but may hold very different effects when used in our schools.
- Summarize the relationship of educational reform to issues of diversity, access, and equity.
- Differentiate among types of leadership and their relationship to access, equity, and diversity.

WAS THERE AN ACHIEVEMENT GAP BEFORE 2002?

Equity and inequity are interconnected. To understand equity, we must know inequity. To fully understand equity is to have deep knowledge of inequities that exist in our society. Let's explore a historical example from recent US education history. Though states like California and Tennessee had begun disaggregating student achievement data by demographic groups[1] well before No Child Left Behind (NCLB) was signed into law by President George W. Bush in 2002, it was NCLB that brought the achievement gap to the forefront of national attention. The question we raise is:

Did the achievement gap exist prior to NCLB or similar state and local initiatives?

Of course it existed. Those of us who were educators prior to 2002 can attest to the existence of achievement disparities, but we can also confirm the resistance to acknowledging and confronting those disparities. In schoolhouses across the country, there were educators who tried to confront colleagues' mindsets that were closed to recognizing achievement

---

1. We use the term *demographic group* instead of the more popular *subgroup* to mitigate the possibility of negative stereotyping. We acknowledge that *subgroup* is a nonpejorative term used by professionals in the assessment community, but we have experienced negative reactions to the term when used with the broader, diverse communities served by our schools and school districts and thereby, respectfully, find *demographic group* to be descriptive and accurate.

disparities and were stonewalled by those who resisted the data. In fact, as a profession we became practiced at deflecting concern for achievement by declaring the causes were beyond us. We blamed poverty, neighborhoods, parents, culture, and often, all of the above. Of course, poverty and other socioeconomic factors are real-world pressures beyond the control of most schools, but they cannot be used to escape our responsibilities to make the hours students are on campus as meaningful as possible.

EDUCATION REFORM IS MORE THAN 150 YEARS OLD

Educational reform has been ongoing for more than 150 years; yet inclusive and equitable practices are recent phenomena. Our intent with this book is to ensure that the CCSS and related reform efforts of the future be transformative at two levels. First, application of the standards are meant to be inclusive of all demographic groups of students as we continue to prepare our students to be ready for careers and higher education. Second, the educators view CCSS as their opportunity and responsibility to change policies and practices in ways that build on the assets students bring to school and avoid stigmatizing cultures as being disadvantaged.

Culturally Proficient mindsets, when considered together, that can foster equitable practices include:

- Educational reform has been on a trajectory of continuous improvement since the middle of the 19th century.
- Our democracy has been evolving since the late 18th century, and our evolution has been accompanied by a continuous expansion of basic civil rights.
- That 21st century schooling is evolving from being a democratization process to being a global competitiveness process is, at best, a false dichotomy.
- Poverty is a conundrum assiduously avoided by government and corporate leaders.
- Quality professional learning by, for, and with educators must be culturally proficient.

For the Common Core to have impact, and for professional development/learning to be effective, equity, access, and inclusion must be embedded into conceptions of the CCSS. With these mindsets in place, educators will be well equipped to embrace and use all future reforms that emanate from government, the private sector, and our own professional efforts.

A BRIEF HISTORY OF INEQUITY AND EQUITY

We can continue to perpetuate historical inequities, or we can lead our organizations to historical levels of effectiveness and achievement. The choice is ours (Lindsey, Roberts, & CampbellJones, 2013). A brief tour through history may demonstrate the extent to which inequity is ingrained in society. Our intent is to support your efforts to identify unrecognized or unacknowledged inequities in your classroom or school in ways that contribute to your Culturally Proficient Professional Learning.

The dubious gift of inequity in the founding documents of the United States begins with the absence of women, African Americans, or First Nations People being included as fully participating citizens. The US Constitution did not provide basic rights to all people, only to property-owning white men. Prominent illustrations of our historical inequities are the following:

- Embedded in the US Constitutions is the 3/5 Compromise whereby slaves were counted as 3/5 of a person for purposes of apportionment in the US House of Representatives and to provide southern states more representatives so as not to be overwhelmed by the more populous northern states.
- Women could not vote in federal elections until 1920 and the passage of the 19th amendment.
- Aboriginal First Nations people were systematically denied basic rights of citizenship.

Many additional examples of such historical inequities exist in our nation's history. At the end of this chapter are recommendations for additional, informative readings on these topics. Our purpose in this chapter is to illustrate that while these historical and frequently brutal experiences were being administered to Americans, there were also efforts pushing for equitable treatment and outcomes that slowly wound their ways through our history. The tenacity of people who could see the true fruits of democracy as revealed by a sentence from the US Declaration of Independence—"We hold these truths to be self-evident, that all men (sic) are created equal, that they are endowed by their Creator with certain unalienable rights, that among these are life, liberty and the pursuit of happiness." These countless faceless people used a variety of legal and quasi-legal avenues to press for changes in society. For example, the women's suffrage movement traces its origins from the founding of the United States and became formalized in the mid-19th century. The abolitionist movement was alive and well during the late 18th century and has roots in 16th century Europe. However, these efforts were slow to develop and take root in ways that transformed society.

In direct contrast to the initial proscriptions of inclusiveness, our founding fathers bequeathed gifts of equity in the founding documents. Whether or not the founding fathers intended to serve the ends of equity and social justice, they included amendatory change processes that allowed our country to evolve in ways not existent in the realities of late 18th century North America. The brilliance of the US Constitution may be found in its "amendment process" as well as the checks and balances system among the three branches of government: legislative, judicial, and executive.

Illustrations of legislative actions:

- The 13th, 14th, and 15th amendments to the US Constitution ended slavery, guaranteed citizenship and equal protection of the law, overturned the 3/5 Compromise, and protected the right to vote. It must be noted that women were still excluded from the right to vote.
- The 19th amendment to the US Constitution guaranteed the right of women to vote.
- The Elementary and Secondary Education Act (1965) and Head Start (1965) were far-reaching efforts as part of President Johnson's War on Poverty. The bills were designed to address inequitable school funding, included mechanisms to address achievement gaps, and fostered highly successful compensatory education programs.

Illustrations of judicial actions:

- The US Supreme Court in a 9-0 vote on *Brown vs. Topeka Board of Education* in 1954 ended legalized segregation.
- The US Supreme Court in *Lau, et al. vs. Nichols, et al.* expanded the rights of English-learning students to education that does not use language as a means to deny or limit equality.
- The US Supreme Court overturned the 1996 Defense of Marriage Act, 2013, protecting the rights of gay and lesbian citizens married in states that supported marriage among same-sex couples.

Illustrations of executive actions:

- President Dwight David Eisenhower's 1957 decision to intervene and countermand Arkansas Governor Orval Faubus's efforts to block the desegregation of Central High School in Little Rock.
- President Harry S. Truman's executive order issued in 1948 effectively desegregating the US military.

During the latter half of the 19th century and throughout the 20th century, basic rights, not initially granted to all people, were gradually expanded in ways that were increasingly inclusive. Though there are numerous success stories throughout this period of time, much work continues to be done. For many African American, Latino, Aboriginal First Nations, and Asian Pacific Island communities, the work seems like it has not touched them. For every illustration of progress, there are illustrations of regression (Beatty, 2012).

REFLECTION

Whether or not you are a student of history, most likely you recognize that historical forces have created the many gifts and challenges that we inherit as educators, let alone as citizens. Now that you have read the section above, what thoughts, reactions, feelings, or questions occur to you? Please use the space below to record your thinking.

MORE ABOUT THE ACHIEVEMENT GAP

Span and Rivers (2012) in their highly important research demonstrate that studying the achievement gap by comparing African American students to white students in any given year both limits and misplaces the needed focus. Their study as educational historians demonstrates the remarkable progress that African American students have made since the 1954 legal dismantling of the apartheid practices of Jim Crow within the United States. The generational academic strides African American students have made in 60 years to overcome 300 years of slavery and legalized segregation is remarkable. Compensatory education programs that flowed out of the Elementary and Secondary Education Act and Head Start in 1965 supported our students across racial, ethnic, and socioeconomic lines. This is a fertile area for further research to conduct similar studies that focus on longitudinal achievement patterns of Latino, Aboriginal First Nations, and Asian Pacific Islander student groups.

Longitudinal, intergenerational studies do not replace year-over-year comparisons, but they can be used to complement annual achievement assessments such as the National Assessment of Educational Progress (NAEP) that too often are used to reinforce the notion of students being "disadvantaged" when in truth these students and their forebears have been underresourced and shortchanged for generations. When we say assessments such as these have been used inappropriately to reinforce negative stereotypes of demographic groups of students, it must be noted that NAEP has been disaggregating assessment data since 1971. So, the achievement gap has been well documented—if, in fact, not well acknowledged. It is, indeed, an understatement to say that an educational debt is owed to racial and ethnic communities who have been targeted by legalized discrimination for generations.

No, this is not easy work. If it were, we wouldn't be writing this book and you would not be reading it seeking resources to support your efforts at continuous improvement. Our collective goal must be to be focused on making substantive changes in a world that too often seeks immediate solutions.

LONG AND NEAR VIEWS: SCHOOL REFORM EFFORTS AND EQUITY

Superfine (2013) in his discussion of how law and policy decisions in our country's history have affected educational equity, notes that it is the processes of implementation that determine the outcome of most reforms. Efforts to reform education are almost as American as apple pie. Public schooling has its roots in pre–Civil War Massachusetts and New York. Efforts to reform and define what is public school and public schooling have continued unabated since that time (Hutt, 2012).

Canada and the United States have histories of inequity that have created educational gaps for underserved student groups. From these histories of inequity are twin forces that intertwine to shape what has occurred and what is to happen in our nation's schools—false dichotomies that lead to the "failure" of public schools and the pressure to reform schools to serve changing global economic conditions.

FALSE DICHOTOMIES AND THE "FAILURE" OF PUBLIC SCHOOLS

Critics of public schools have taken to using false dichotomies such as "School Reform" **or** "Continuous Improvement" and "Democratization" **or** "Global Competitiveness," leading to the assumption of the failure of public schools. Most importantly, public schools are not failing. Students whose demographic counterparts were doing well in the 1960s and 1970s are doing as well if not better in the 21st century. The latter half of the 20th century witnessed a broader range of demographic groups attending high school because of state-level initiatives requiring compulsory education. In this context, school reform of the latter part of the 20th century into the 21st century revealed a demographic profile of more students from lower socioeconomic groups attending and graduating from high school. In this context, reform measures that included more diverse student populations often did not consider students' cultures as assets but more as "disadvantages" to be corrected (Borrero, Yeh, Crivir, & Suda, 2012; Lindsey, Karns, & Myatt, 2010).

An unintended consequence of the phrase "school reform" may be that the term is fraught with problems that often undercut any intended good outcomes. To *reform* something connotes to improve it and sends the message, intended or otherwise, that what is currently being done is not right or is ineffective. In too many instances, those—people or schools—being reformed don't see a need to change and are content with current practice. School desegregation sent a very clear message to society that the education of African American students was not effective in segregated settings. Then, as a nation we witnessed massive resistance, first in the South, and, ultimately, throughout the United States. Yes, there were islands of support for desegregation or integration; however, those success stories did not capture national attention in ways that advanced equity on a national basis.

As many of the nation's schools continued to struggle with educating African American students, many educators believed that schools were being blamed for the failure of society to correct the inequities created by more than 300 years of slavery and Jim Crow practices. As the national consciousness was being raised about racial disparities, our nation became increasingly aware of other systemic inequities affecting female students, English learning students, special need students, and Native American and First Nation students.

The "failure" of public schools to successfully address these systemic, societal issues in a generation or two has become the rallying cry for "reforming" public education to do what the general society has not had the stomach to do, which is to create conditions for an egalitarian society. The 1954 US Supreme Court decision *Brown v. Board of Education* ushered in an era of multiple school reform movements that sought to prepare students for democratic citizenship (a public purpose) and to give students an equal opportunity for social mobility (a private goal; Spencer, 2013). These twin goals led to the following and other legal actions:

- Desegregation (US Civil Rights Acts, 1964, 1965),
- School finance reform (*Serrano v. Priest,* 1971, 1976, 1977), and
- Laws and policies to protect the rights of English language learners and students with disabilities (*Lau v. Nichols,* 1974, and Pub. L. No. 94-145, 1975).

Had we as a nation embraced and committed to generational continuous improvement, as Span and Rivers (2012) discovered, the mindset of demographic groups being capable of high academic success would have been realized. The good news is that it is not too late for all students to experience success. Student success will come when educators hold a commitment to believing our students are capable of learning at high levels and that we are capable of teaching all students. Year-over-year comparisons may have some benefits, but not when those data are used to stigmatize demographic groups of students as being disadvantaged when, truth be told, their progress, given generational and systemic inequities, is remarkable.

SCHOOL REFORM IN A TIME OF CHANGING WORLDWIDE ECONOMIC CONDITIONS

The presidency of Ronald Reagan in the 1980s witnessed a pivotal turning point in which international economic competition expanded in unprecedented ways. Suddenly, the United States was faced with a need for workers who could fulfill the technology demands of the new workforce; the industrial factory model was dead, buried, kaput! The goals of public schools shifted from preparing students for democratic citizenship to preparing them to work in fast-paced, nimble companies that were competing with comparatively low-wage foreign workforces, even in high-tech industries.

As the national and competing international economies were rapidly evolving and becoming more technology-based, opposition to court-mandated school reform efforts led to institutional changes, especially the rise of state legislative and executive activity and a strong ethos of "local control." Above all, these changes went hand in hand with a concept of equality that changed in three ways:

- From the protection of rights to the reform of whole school systems that were thought to have produced inequalities in the first place;
- From equality of inputs (funding, access to schools and programs) to an emphasis on educational outcomes as measured by standardized tests; and
- From sameness to the notion that all students should receive at least an *adequate* education, defined in relation to standards (Spencer, 2013; Superfine, 2013).

These views of equity fostered reforms intended to change what was wrong with students and/or schools in a matter of a few years. When results were not forthcoming, once again, some politicians and prominent business leaders declared the failure of public schools. Our intent is not to weigh the relative merits of these initiatives but to point out that generational issues are not met with overnight change requirements. Illustrations of current reform efforts that focus on providing near-term results include:

- Standards-based reform and accountability policies, NCLB, and benefits of demographic data (i.e., not "sub" group),
- School choice and vouchers, and
- More robust forms of teacher evaluation (Spencer, 2013) and administrator evaluation (The Regional Equity Assistance Centers, 2013).

We implore school leaders to continue to press for long-range initiatives with periodic/annual benchmarks that focus on continuous improvement to narrow and close achievement gaps. Policymakers at local, state, and national levels must ensure long-term equitable funding and access to broadband technology as fundamental for low-income communities and necessary for all students to be ready for college and career choices (Gjaja, Puckett, & Ryder, 2014; Polis & Gibson, 2014).

CULTURALLY PROFICIENT LEADERSHIP

Leadership in the context of our diverse population and our history of systemic inequity must hold equity, access, and inclusion as core values to guide nonformal and formal school leaders. As you proceed to the next chapter, you will learn that the Guiding Principles of Cultural Proficiency represent equity, access, and inclusion as central values. For the CCSS or any other reform effort to have long-term impact across demographic groups, the Cultural Proficiency framework needs to be embedded into conceptions of school leadership that effectively benefit all students.

Being a culturally proficient educator is to understand the concepts of entitlement and privilege and their relationship to systems of oppression. Racism and other forms of oppression exist only because the dominant group benefits from the continued practices. This is not a zero-sum game where if one side gains, another has to lose. Culturally proficient educational leaders shift their thinking and are intentional in understanding both the negative consequences of oppression as well as the manner in which people benefit from those same systems. Culturally proficient leaders allocate human and fiscal resources to equitably benefit all students.

Transforming schools to be effective in educating historically marginalized students involves confronting power at two levels—the individual educator and the school as a system. Culturally proficient educators embrace their personal power and their schools' institutional authority to address organizational barriers and use their power to transform policies and practices. Weick (1979) contends that organization is a myth and that "most 'things' in organizations are actually relationships tied together in systematic fashion" (p. 88). In other words, we invent social organizations through our interactions with one another. As you will read in Chapter 3, the extremes of Cultural Destructiveness and Cultural Proficiency are similarly invented ways of organizing our social interactions, which once again, is a choice we are to make.

Leadership requires a mindset that change is a process to be managed. Shields (2010), as presented in Chapter 1, described leadership as a progression of three ever-deepening change processes—transactional, transformational, and transformative. Each type of leadership is needed in our schools, but it is transformative leadership that embraces concepts of equity and access in serving the needs of our diverse communities. Culturally proficient education exists within the context of our moral authority as educational leaders. Culturally Proficient leaders ensure that professional learning is focused on the moral imperative of equitable outcomes. Culturally Proficient Professional Learning involves three aspects of our moral authority:

- Recognizing the dynamics of entitlement and privilege,
- Recognizing that our schools contribute to disparities in achievement, and
- Believing that educators can make choices that positively affect student success (Lindsey, Roberts, & CampbellJones, 2013).

Cultural Proficiency requires a leadership perspective that involves an inside-out approach to personal and organizational change. Culturally proficient leaders redefine education in a democracy to be inclusive. These leaders focus on inequity and equity, regardless of who is benefiting from the current status. They focus on confronting and changing one's own behavior to learning from and how to serve the educational needs of new groups in the community, rather than how to change and assimilate members of target groups. Culturally proficient leaders expect criticism from influential people, and they operate in school districts by remaining centered on the moral value in our work as educators.

GOING DEEPER

Take a few moments and think about your thinking. What is occurring to you? In what ways does the information in this chapter inform your thinking? In what ways does the chapter challenge your thinking? What new questions do you have that you may not have had before reading this chapter? Think about your own school or school district. To what extent do you recognize illustrations of inequity and equity? What might be some examples? What questions do you have about your classroom or school? Please use the space below to record your thinking.

_____

_____

_____

_____

DIALOGIC ACTIVITY

With a group of your colleagues, engage in a dialogue to reach shared understanding of *a school culture in support of all learners performing at levels higher than ever before.* What might be some collective mindsets in your school that need to be examined and challenged? To what extent are you as a group willing to step forward? What would be the risk for you? What is the risk for your students if you choose not to? For transformative change to occur for you and your school, what data are readily available that would paint a picture of your school's ethnic/racial, gender, and social-economic diversity. What is your prediction of the picture as it represents student access to higher level thinking experiences, to creative thinking/writing, and to academic success? Use the space below to record your current thinking. Your thoughtful dialogue about these questions will deepen the usefulness of this book as you proceed through the remaining chapters.

_____

_____

_____

_____

_____

_____

This chapter described the dynamics of inequity that exist within our society and, by extension, into our schools. Chapter 3 provides a rich description and discussion of the Tools of Cultural Proficiency that will support your and your school's journey to mitigate and eliminate barriers to student access and achievement.

FOR FURTHER READING ON TOPICS FROM THIS CHAPTER

Banks, James A. (2006). *Race, culture and education: The selected works of James A. Banks.* New York, NY: Routledge.

Miller, Neil. (2006). *Out of the past: Gay and lesbian history from 1869 to the present.* New York, NY: Alyson Books.

Nieto, Sonia, & Bode, Patty. (2012). *Affirming diversity: The sociopolitical context of multicultural education* (6th ed.). Boston, MA: Pearson.

Spencer, John. (2013, August 22). Equality in education law and policy, 1954–2010. *Teachers College Record.* Retrieved from http://www.tcrecord ID Number: 17222.

Superfine, Benjamin Michael. (2013). *Equality in education law and policy, 1954–2010.* New York, NY: Cambridge University Press.

3 The Tools of Cultural Proficiency[1]

Rich American kids do fine; poor American kids don't.

—Alfie Kohn (Straus, 2013, p. 2)

GETTING CENTERED

The history of the United States has been one of an unfolding of the democracy. Access to formal education, particularly in the latter part of the 20th century, was fertile ground for expansion of civil rights in ways that could equip all citizens to participate in the economic, social, and political fruits of this still evolving society. While segregation still endures across the country, there also persist numerous efforts to mitigate and overcome segregation's harmful effects, whether that segregation was intentional or unintentional. The Tools of Cultural Proficiency provide both the individual educator and the school system with a framework and a hands-on means for educating all children and youth to high levels of attainment. The journey to Cultural Proficiency begins in effective communication with self and with colleagues.

Culturally proficient educators engage in personal reflection on their practice as well as become involved in dialogue with colleagues, students,

---

[1]AUTHORS' NOTE: For purposes of consistency, material in this chapter is adapted from earlier Cultural Proficiency books, most recently, Randall B. Lindsey, Richard M. Diaz, Kikanza Nuri-Robins, Raymond D. Terrell, and Delores B. Lindsey, *A Culturally Proficient Response to LGBT Communities: A Guide for Educators, 2013*; Reyes L. Quezada, Delores B. Lindsey, & Randall B. Lindsey, *Culturally Proficient Practice: Supporting Educators of English Learning Students, 2012;* and Randall B. Lindsey, Kikanza Nuri-Robins, & Raymond D. Terrell, *Cultural Proficiency: A Manual for School Leaders, 2009.*

and parents/guardians about shared educational and community interests. In our work with school districts across the United States and Canada, we have learned that people and organizations who are effective in cross-cultural communication regularly engage in "thinking about their own thinking" and in "seeking to understand others"—two skills basic to Cultural Proficiency's "inside-out" approach to individual and organizational change.

Take a few minutes to think and respond to the following questions:

- What was your initial response to the phrases—*personal reflection on practice?*
- What was your initial response to *cross-cultural dialogue with colleagues, students, and parents/guardians?*
- To what degree are you involved with your colleagues in conversations about educating all learners?
- What might be some ways in which you are engaged in thinking about your own learning?

_____

_____

_____

_____

REFLECTION AND DIALOGUE ENHANCE THINKING

Reflection and dialogue used in mindful and consistent ways are indispensable communication devices that support effective uses of the Tools of Cultural Proficiency. Schools are complex organizations composed of countless formal and informal communications networks. Our experiences have been that when educators intentionally and purposefully use reflection and dialogue, they contribute to healthy school environments for themselves and their students. The intersection of reflection and dialogue with Cultural Proficiency provides benefits:

- For individuals, the Tools of Cultural Proficiency guide reflection to recognize and understand barriers that impede your and your students' learning as well as core values that support and facilitate learning. Later in this chapter we describe Overcoming Barriers to Cultural Proficiency as critical to being an effective educator. Once barriers are evident to educators, continued reflective practice guides use of your and your students' cultural assets to sustain learning.
- For groups composed of any combination of teachers, administrators, counselors, trustee/board members, or any persons interested

in educational issues, the Tools of Cultural Proficiency provide the opportunity for dialogue to lead to understanding individual and organizational cultures in the school. Similar to reflection, dialogue allows groups to recognize barriers to their and their students learning and to purposefully embrace core values that view culture as assets, not deficits.

This intentional and purposeful combination of personal reflection and organizational dialogue leads to a healthy state we call the inside-out process of change. The focus of the change process is on shifting thinking and changing conversations from viewing culture as a deficiency to viewing culture as an asset.

SINEK—*WHY?* IN ADDITION TO *HOW?* OR *WHEN?*

Simon Sinek (2009) indicates that effective action occurs when leaders inspire others through posing *why* questions. It is incumbent for leaders to recognize that fellow educators, like their students, are not interchangeable widgets that lend themselves to reductionist sets of how-to activities. The legacy of current educational reform movements, if nothing else, maybe taught us *how* to do things and *when* to do them. The mantras of educational reform have led teachers across the country knowing *how* to construct various forms of lesson plans, administrators knowing *how* to look for the seven steps in an "effective lesson plan," and both knowing *when* testing is to occur.

Though there is a most important role for the *how* and *when* questions, they are made more meaningful, particularly when planning for change that involves diversity, equity, and access to pose the morally laden *why* questions. Cultural Proficiency is an inside-out process of change that values *why* questions.

REFLECTION AND DIALOGUE LEAD TO INSIDE-OUT CHANGE

Culturally proficient practices, whether individual or organizational, are developed through intentional willingness to examine our own behavior and values as well as our school's (or district/board's) policies and practices. Examinations such as these are facilitated through the use of two communication devices referenced above—personal reflection and dialogue. Now that you have thought about and recorded your reaction to these two terms, let's take a look at how we believe these two communication techniques support your learning.

- *Reflection*—The conversation we have with ourselves that leads to even deeper understanding of our own values and beliefs. Sustained reflection often entails exploration of the cultural bases for one's belief systems and for "why" we do the things we do.
- *Dialogue*—The conversation we have with others to understand their values and beliefs. The emphasis is on "understanding" others and not on making decisions, or solving problems, or trying to convince others of the errors of their ways. Dialogue that explores organizational or institutional understanding seeks to explore the bases for stated policies and prevalent practices. Exploration into organizational policies and practices almost always finds that the initial reason given for current policies and practices is "well, it's always the way we have done it here." True, sustained dialogue seeks to go deeper to understand and explore the historical and/or cultural bases for policies and practices. The deeper dialogue helps members of the organization surface deeply held assumptions that have guided decisions and historically determined distribution of resources. Without exposing these assumptions, status quo continues without question or exposure. The questions, "Why do we do what we do?" and "Are we who we say we are?" are the questions that most often help surface deeply and long-held assumptions.

Educators who use the communication skills of reflection and dialogue to learn and apply the Tools of Cultural Proficiency are well positioned to provide effective high-level educational opportunities and outcomes for historically marginalized students, educators, and parents/community members. In the hands of a skilled practitioner, the Tools of Cultural Proficiency enable you to intentionally change your practices and the policies and practices of your school in ways that better serve the educational needs of your diverse communities and, in doing so, also serve dominant group members in more authentic ways.

To illustrate the importance and use of reflection and dialogue, we share with you an e-mail from Sarah Gazan, a colleague in Manitoba, who presented an introductory overview of Cultural Proficiency to a professional group. After the session, she sent this e-mail to one of the authors to illustrate her personal reflection that led to an inside-out growth experience that affected her and her daughter as well as a dialogue with her daughter, Hannah, that further deepened her personal learning. As you read her e-mail, think of how you might respond if you were an educator serving the needs of Sarah, Hannah, and their family.

The one lady had a concern about it (i.e., Cultural Proficiency) being "the new thing," . . . but I explained that it's not new to education and not even to Manitoba as Manitoba Family Services and Housing has mandatory Culture and Diversity and Building Inclusive Environments training for all social workers in the province. . . That seemed to answer her question. I found a really awesome quote about how everything someone thinks, knows, does, believes is based on culture and you can't understand student performance unless you understand the cultural context. 'If cultural differences aren't considered then we run the risk of identifying simple difference as serious deficits.' I started with a story I wanted to share with you.

When I was preparing for this presentation I started to think about my mother. My mom always talked to me about how the hardest journey was the one you made from your head to your heart. She also said that if you found the courage to make that journey, that was how you changed yourself and made the world a better place in a good way. I think what my mom taught me is important to what we are talking about today because cultural proficiency is really about making that courageous journey from your head to your heart to make our schools and our communities a better place for students and families. I just wanted to share a personal story about my own journey. My daughter was learning about living and nonliving things in her science class. One day she came home and was very upset because part of a classroom activity was to classify objects into two categories, living and nonliving. When she came to a rock, she placed it in the living category because from Cree worldview rocks are grandfathers and have a spirit and so they are considered to be living. From a Western perspective, it's a rock, and a rock is a rock. That night as we talked, I told my daughter that there were some things that she had to learn for school that were different from home but that it was important that she learn it for her science class. She responded by saying, "But, Mom, why don't they think Cree people are important?" I started to think about my response to my daughter and I realised the terrible message that I was sending her, our values and beliefs were not important. That is when I began my journey from my head to my heart because I knew I had a responsibility as a teacher and as a parent to ensure that my daughter and my students received an education that acknowledged and valued different ways of knowing and where my daughter could maintain her identity as Cree person.

REFLECTION

Take a moment and think about Sarah's conversation with Hannah. In what ways does Sarah's depiction of her conversation with Hannah demonstrate reflection and dialogue? In what ways might the conversation provide an illustration of Sinek's posing the "why" question?

_____

_____

_____

_____

_____

_____

THE TOOLS OF CULTURAL PROFICIENCY

The Tools of Cultural Proficiency enable you to do the following:

- Describe Barriers to Cultural Proficiency you may have experienced or observed that impede cultural proficiency.
- Describe how the Guiding Principles of Cultural Proficiency serve as core values for your personal, professional, and organizational values and behavior.
- Describe unhealthy and healthy values and behaviors and school policies and practices and plot them on the Cultural Proficiency Continuum.
- Describe and use the 5 Essential Elements of Cultural Competence as standards for your personal and professional behavior and your school's formal policies and nonformal, prevalent practices.

THE CONCEPTUAL FRAMEWORK IS A GUIDE

The conceptual framework illustrates the manner in which cultural assets form the basis for core values to guide educational leaders. Recognizing and understanding the tension that exists for people and schools in terms of barriers versus assets prepares you to better serve the students in your classroom, school and district.

Table 3.1 presents the Conceptual Framework of Cultural Proficiency and shows the four Tools of Cultural Proficiency and the relationship among the tools. Begin by reading Table 3.1 from the bottom up. Please regard reading in this fashion as a cultural experience.

BARRIERS VERSUS CULTURAL ASSETS: THE TENSION FOR CHANGE

The Barriers to Cultural Proficiency and the Guiding Principles (e.g., core values) of Cultural Proficiency are the "invisible guiding hands" of the framework. Barriers inform the negative aspects of the Continuum—Cultural Destructiveness, Incapacity and Blindness, while the Guiding Principles serve to inform the positive aspects of the Continuum—Precompetence, Competence, and Proficiency. Being able to recognize and acknowledge the Barriers to Cultural Proficiency is basic to understanding how to overcome resistance to change within us and in our

Table 3.1 The Cultural Proficiency Framework

THE ESSENTIAL ELEMENTS—Standards for Planning and Evaluating

- **Assess Culture:** Identify the cultural groups present in the system
- **Value Diversity:** Develop an appreciation for the differences among and between groups
- **Manage the Dynamics of Difference:** Learn to respond appropriately and effectively to the issues that arise in a diverse environment
- **Adapt to Diversity:** Change and adopt new policies and practices that support diversity and inclusion
- **Institutionalize Cultural Knowledge:** Drive the changes into the systems of the organization

Cultural Proficiency Continuum

Change Mandated for Tolerance			Change Chosen for Transformation		
Destruction	Incapacity	Blindness	Precompetence	Competence	Proficiency
Eliminate differences	*Demean differences*	*Dismiss differences*	*Respond inadequately to the dynamics of difference*	*Engage with differences using the essential elements as standards*	*Esteem and learn from differences as a lifelong practice*
The elimination of other people's cultures	Belief in the superiority of one's culture and behavior that disempowers another's culture	Acting as if the cultural differences you see do not matter or not recognizing that there are differences among and between cultures	Awareness of the limitations of one's skills or an organization's practices when interacting with other cultural groups	Using the 5 Essential Elements of Cultural Proficiency as the standard for individual behavior and organizational practices	Knowing how to learn about and from individual and organizational culture; interacting effectively in a variety of cultural environments; advocating for others

Reactive Behaviors, Shaped by the BARRIERS

- Unawareness of the need to adapt
- Resistance to change
- Systems of oppression and privilege
- A sense of entitlement

Proactive Behaviors, Shaped by the PRINCIPLES

- Culture is a predominant force in people's and school's lives.
- People are served in varying degrees by the dominant culture.
- People have group identities and individual identities.
- Diversity within cultures is vast and significant.
- Each cultural group has unique cultural needs.
- The best of both worlds enhances the capacity of all.
- The family, as defined by each culture, is the primary system of support in the education of children.
- School systems must recognize that marginalized populations have to be at least bicultural and that this status creates a unique set of issues to which the system must be equipped to respond.
- Inherent in cross-cultural interactions are dynamics that must be acknowledged, adjusted to, and accepted.

schools. From Table 3.1, you learned there are barriers to culturally proficient attitudes, behaviors, policies, and practices that affect our daily lives and impact educational leaders' decisions (Cross, 1989; Lindsey, Nuri Robins, & Terrell, 2009):

- Being resistant to change
- Being unaware of the need to adapt
- Not acknowledging systemic oppression
- Benefitting from a sense of privilege and entitlement

Notice the line between the Barriers and the Guiding Principles. That line extends between Cultural Blindness and Cultural Precompetence and represents the paradigmatic shifting point where educators have clearly delineated choices:

- To the left of the line, people choose to be a victim of social forces and to believe either in cultural deficit theory applied to marginalized communities or, ever bit as damaging, the intractability of systemic oppression visited on marginalized communities; or
- To the right of the line, people choose to believe in their capacity to effectively educate all students, irrespective of their racial, ethnic, gender, socioeconomic, sexual identity, special needs, or faith communities.

The Guiding Principles of Cultural Proficiency function as a counter to the Barriers to Cultural Proficiency by serving as core values in developing our capacity for personal and professional work that results in marginalized students being academically successful and full participants in the extracurricular programs of the school. Culture is inculcated in the guiding principles and can be readily seen in our behaviors, policies, and practices. Let us be direct and specific: to be effective, the core values must be deeply held beliefs and values. They cannot and must not be lightly agreed to in nodding assent and, then, blithely ignored. The Guiding Principles inform our actions for being Cultural Precompetent, Cultural Competent, and Cultural Proficient. The Guiding Principles are as follows:

- Culture is a predominant force in people's and school's lives.
- People are served in varying degrees by the dominant culture.
- People have group identities and individual identities.
- Diversity within cultures is vast and significant.
- Each cultural group has unique cultural needs.

- The best of both worlds enhances the capacity of all.
- The family, as defined by each culture, is the primary system of support in the education of children.
- School systems must recognize that marginalized populations have to be at least bicultural and that this status creates a unique set of issues to which the system must be equipped to respond.
- Inherent in cross-cultural interactions are dynamics that must be acknowledged, adjusted to, and accepted.

TRANSFORMING THE CULTURE OF SCHOOL

Of all the cultural groups that schools serve, the organizational culture of school is the group that most often is the focus of "change, or needs to be changed." Organizational and school culture has been studied extensively even in recent years. Researchers concur that schools as organizations have a culture of their own and need leaders who understand and manage that culture in a positive way (Deal & Kennedy, 1982; Fullan, 2003; Schein, 2010; Wagner et al., 2006). Both veteran and new educators acknowledge that change is not easy. Within schools abide forces that either block (Barriers) or facilitate (Guiding Principles) student achievement. Implementing new practices in schools is often difficult and made even more difficult when issues serving the educational needs of marginalized students are embedded in change processes. While it may be true that change is not easy, we know also that change is inevitable and natural. When properly understood and implemented, a change initiative such as the Common Core State Standards can be led in ways that target the educational needs of traditionally underserved students and, at the same time, benefit all learners in our schools. Cultural Proficiency does not focus on struggling learners and ignore high-achieving students. Culturally proficient educators create classroom and schoolwide conditions that support all learners achieving at levels higher than even before.

Formal and nonformal school leaders must be able to recognize and acknowledge personal and institutional barriers to creating conditions for teaching and learning while advocating for practices that benefit all students, schools, and districts. The Conceptual Framework of Cultural Proficiency is a mental model for managing change that we use to understand and tell our stories in ways that may inform you as you continue your journey to increased effectiveness as an educator (Dilts, 1990, 1994; Lindsey, Nuri Robins, Terrell, 2009; Senge et al., 2000).

REGARDING CULTURE AS AN ASSET LEADS TO CULTURAL PROFICIENCY

The Cultural Proficiency Continuum and Essential Elements of Cultural Proficiency are the visible Tools of Cultural Proficiency and are represented by what we do, not by what we say we do. The Essential Elements are standards for personal and professional behavior as well as for organizational policies and practices. As noted above, the Guiding Principles are core values that inform and guide the Essential Elements. When culture is embraced as an asset, educational successes can be crafted, both for ourselves as educators and for the communities we serve. Tables 3.2 and 3.3 describe in greater detail the phases of the Cultural Proficiency Continuum and the Essential Elements of Cultural Competence.

Table 3.2, The Cultural Proficiency Continuum—Depicting Unhealthy and Healthy Practices, aligns the six phases of Cultural Proficiency so you can see clearly that the Barriers to Cultural Proficiency inform Cultural Destructiveness, Incapacity and Blindness. These phases are, at best, half-hearted compliance-driven behaviors that rarely result in actions to support the academic and social success of historically marginalized students or the effective inclusion of historically marginalized colleagues and community members. In marked contrast, the Guiding Principles of Cultural Proficiency serve as core values to support Culturally Precompetent, Competent and Proficient behaviors, policies and practices for students, educators, and parents/community members by esteeming their cultures.

Table 3.3 displays The Essential Elements of Cultural Competence. This is the point on the Continuum "where the action is." Our caution to you is that blind adherence to these five standards without a full understanding of the Barriers and Guiding Principles will, most assuredly, lead to frustration. Being equipped with effective teaching and leadership strategies that honor and recognize diverse communities combined with the view that our students' cultures are assets on which to build a relationship, you will be better prepared and less frustrated to meet the academic and social needs of historically marginalized students. Take a moment and study Table 3.3, The Essential Elements of Cultural Competence, and ask in what ways these "actions" might inform your practice.

LEVELS OF COMMITMENT TO CHANGE AND IMPROVEMENT

In this section, our discussion of large-scale change initiatives is adapted from a previously cited publication, *Culturally Proficient Coaching:*

Table 3.2 The Cultural Proficiency Continuum—Depicting Unhealthy and Healthy Practices

Cultural Destructiveness	Cultural Incapacity	Cultural Blindness	Cultural Precompetence	Cultural Competence	Cultural Proficiency
Compliance-Based Tolerance for Diversity			*Transformation for Equity*		

Compliance-Based Tolerance for Diversity

- **Cultural Destructiveness**—Seeking to eliminate references to the culture of "others" in all aspects of the school and in relationship with their communities.
- **Cultural Incapacity**—Trivializing "other" communities and seeking to make them appear to be wrong.
- **Cultural Blindness**—Pretending not to see or acknowledge the status and culture of marginalized communities and choosing to ignore the experiences of such groups within the school and community.

Transformation for Equity

- **Cultural Precompetence**—Increasingly aware of what you and the school don't know about working with marginalized communities. It is at this key level of development that you and the school can move in a positive, constructive direction or you can vacillate, stop, and possibly regress.
- **Cultural Competence**—Manifesting your personal values and behaviors and the school's policies and practices in a manner that is inclusive with marginalized cultures and communities that are new or different from you and the school.
- **Cultural Proficiency**—Advocating for lifelong learning for the purpose of being increasingly effective in serving the educational needs of the cultural groups served by the school. Holding the vision that you and the school are instruments for creating a socially just democracy.

Source: Adapted from Raymond D. Terrell and Randall B. Lindsey. (2009). *Culturally Proficient Leadership: The Personal Journey Begins Within.* Thousand Oaks, CA: Corwin.

Table 3.3 The Essential Elements of Cultural Competence

- **Assessing Cultural Knowledge**—Become aware of and know the diverse communities within your school; know how educators and the school as a whole react to marginalized communities and learn how to be effective in serving these communities. Leads and learns about the school and its grade levels and departments as cultural entities in responding to the educational needs of the underserved communities.
- **Valuing Diversity**—Creating informal and formal decision-making groups inclusive of parents/guardians and community members whose viewpoints and experiences are different from yours and the dominant group at the school, and that will enrich conversations, decision making, and problem solving.
- **Managing the Dynamics of Difference**—Modeling problem-solving and conflict-resolution strategies as a natural and normal process within the culture of the school and the diverse contexts of the communities of your school.
- **Adapting to Diversity**—Learning about underserved cultural groups different from your own and the ability to use others' experiences and backgrounds in all school settings.
- **Institutionalizing Cultural Knowledge**—Making learning about underserved cultural groups and their experiences and perspectives an integral part of the school's professional development.

Source: Adapted from Raymond D. Terrell and Randall B. Lindsey. (2009). *Culturally Proficient Leadership: The Personal Journey Begins Within*. Thousand Oaks, CA: Corwin.

Supporting Educators to Create Equitable Schools (Lindsey, Martinez, & Lindsey, 2007). We reference this work here because the degree of commitment to a change initiative that a school or district holds is often the primary indicator of success or failure in reaching its student performance goals. The level of commitment is reflected in the educators' public rhetoric, the resources (i.e., inclusive of time, people, money, materials) assigned to the initiative, their widely held beliefs that the initiative can produce desired results, the overall efforts to sustain growth over time, and the ability of teachers and leaders to identify change initiatives as part of *the way we do things around* here. Robert Garmston and Bruce Wellman expanded the work of Gregory Bateson and Robert Dilts by developing a model of intervention based on *the nested levels of learning* (Garmston & Wellman, 1999). Table 3.4 shows the "nested level" model of behavioral and organizational change. We offer this model for consideration and implementation of the CCSS.

The nested-level change model (Table 3.4) displays that behavioral and observable changes most significantly occur when all levels are addressed. Change that occurs at one level impacts behaviors below that

Table 3.4   Nested Levels of Organizational Change

Identity: The individual or group's sense of self

Answers the questions: *Who are we? or Who am I?*

> **Belief System: The individual or group's values, beliefs, assumptions, and meanings**
>
> Answers the question: *Why do we do what we do?*
>
> > **Capabilities: The individual and group's reflective and dialogic skills to use new knowledge, understanding, and skills**
> >
> > Answers the question: *How will we develop and use the skills that we have?*
> >
> > > **Behaviors: The individual or group's actions and reactions**
> > >
> > > Answers the question: *In what specific behaviors will I or we engage?*
> > >
> > > > **Environment: Basic physical surroundings, tools, materials, supplies, technology**
> > > >
> > > > Answers the question: *What do we need to begin?*

Source: Adapted from Delores B. Lindsey, Richard S. Martinez, and Randall B. Lindsey. (2007). *Culturally Proficient Coaching: Supporting Educators to Create Equitable Schools.* Thousand Oaks, CA: Corwin.

level (i.e., allocation of resources, decision making, problem solving, professional development, assessment, curriculum, and instruction decisions). Consequently, interventions that happen only at the lower levels do not impact or influence the levels above, thereby lessening the chances or opportunities for large-scale changes.

To illustrate how this model works, we only need to look at school improvement efforts that begin at the two lowest levels such as providing or improving facilities, purchasing materials of instruction, and implementing new academic programs as mandated by local, state, or federal agencies. Often educators and leaders view this method of *change* or improvement as *the answer* to the problem of the student achievement. Although these intervention programs are important and necessary, they often become what we call "fill-in-the-blank" responses to problems, issues, or needs. New programs or interventions are often seen as the solution to improving student achievement even before student data or student needs are analyzed and appropriate questions asked. An example of this *fill-in-the-blank* reform model is:

- *Afterschool tutoring programs will solve the academic problems experienced by students, or*
- *Longer class periods will solve the problem for those students.*

Often, the *what* question is answered before the *why* question is asked.

To follow this logic a bit further, we invite educators to ask this question:

- *If, _____ is the answer, what was the question?*

Was the question about student achievement and demographic groups? What data do we have, or do we need, that shows the depth of the issue? Did we select the program because of the students' needs reflected in our data? What assumptions were made about historically marginalized groups before data were collected? What might be other data that we need to examine?

Implementation decisions for CCSS are to be based on student achievement and participation data, and they are to involve educators in collaboratively selecting intervention programs, developing instructional techniques, and designing assessment strategies that reflect student needs. Middletown Unified School District educators have been engaged in collaborative conversations and data dialogues as part of their districtwide reform efforts to support all students, educators, and parents/community members. The case stories in Chapters 6 through 10 demonstrate the nested levels of commitment to large-scale change in the district.

CULTURALLY PROFICIENT LEADERSHIP LINKS BEHAVIORS WITH BELIEFS AND IDENTITY

Organizational change initiatives that focus on the lower nested levels of behaviors and environments fall short of impacting long-term change, whereas districts that begin change initiatives at the top of the nested-level model have a greater chance of impacting the classroom environment (i.e., lowest level) based on the influence and impact of all other levels, including the organizational identity, widely held belief systems, and skills and capabilities of organizational members (Table 3.4). Cultural Proficiency is an approach that occurs at the upper levels of identity and belief systems and serves to ensure equity considerations in implementation of CCSS. The Tools for Cultural Proficiency guide individuals and organizations to examine their values and behaviors based on their beliefs and assumptions about how students learn and who can learn. This is the *inside-out approach* for changing behaviors and environments. Once an organization's members examine who they are and for whose purpose they exist (**Vision and Identity**), they have a greater chance of developing skills and **capabilities**

Table 3.5 Nested Levels: Leverage Points for Implementation of CCSS

Middletown Unified School District (MUSD) board/trustees and superintendent promote the district identity as high-performing academically, with student-centered instruction and community engagement. The result of the district's focus is an inclusive and cohesive district goal and community-wide vision aligned with Common Core State Standards.

Answers the question: *Who are we?*

Superintendent's leadership cabinet hosts conversations/professional learning focused on districtwide mission, core values, belief statements, and public agreements. These agreements are aligned with the board's goals and district vision statement/identity.

Answers the question: *Why do we do what we do?*

District office and site leaders demonstrate high value for professional learning that supports teachers and leaders by providing this book to engage teachers, counselors, administrators, paraprofessionals, parents/guardians, and community members in effective educational practices.

Answers the question: *How will we develop new skills and/or use the skills that we have?*

MUSD educators adopt a well-defined plan of standards-based curriculum, instruction, and assessment aligned with languages, academic needs, and cultural backgrounds of students. Educators engage in comprehensive, culturally proficient, professional learning focused on needs of historically underserved students as well as educators and parents/community members.

Answers the question: *In what specific behaviors will we engage?*

School site educators create supportive conditions, provide facilities, resources, and appropriate materials to engage educators in implementing standards-based curriculum, instruction, and assessment.

Answers the question: *What do we need to begin?*

Source: Adapted from Garmston and Wellman (1999, 2013).

to address the behaviors and **environments** within the organization. Once programs are consistent with the organization's identity and beliefs, group members share the responsibility of developing **resources** in support of those agreed upon initiatives. Middletown Unified School District is an example of members employing nested levels of organizational change.

MIDDLETOWN UNIFIED SCHOOL DISTRICT: A CASE STORY

Middletown Unified School District (MUSD) has been on a journey toward creating a culturally proficient environment so that educators can ensure students in the district are working toward meeting Common Core State Standards and being prepared for college and career. Middletown is a composite narrative of many districts in Canada and the United States with whom we authors have worked as presenters and facilitators. In Chapters 7 through 11, we present narratives called "case stories." The intent of the case story is to give you a true-to-life situation for you to be the "observer." Rather than ask you to analyze the case as in the typical case study format, we ask you to "reflect-on-action" and "reflect-for-action." We ask you to use the lens of Cultural Proficiency and reflect on what you think and what you might do as a result of your reflection.

In the case stories, educators from Middletown engage in conversations that illustrate how Cultural Proficiency supports the standards-based, student-centered educational system. Table 3.5 illustrates how the MUSD board and superintendent along with community leaders make high expectations, rigorous curriculum, and instructional integrity explicit in policies and practices throughout the organization.

MUSD has acknowledged that the practice of Culturally Proficient programs is grounded in the district's identity as a high-performing, student-centered system. A quick review of Table 3.5 illustrates how change or clarity at the highest level of identity cascades throughout the organization. Now, take the Middletown story with you when you read Chapters 7 through 11 to enhance your skills using the Tools of Cultural Proficiency.

GOING DEEPER

Take a few minutes to think and respond to the following questions:

- In what ways has this chapter informed and supported your learning about reflection?

- How has this chapter informed and supported your understanding about the Tools Cultural Proficiency?
- How has your thinking about teaching and interacting with students, educators, and parents/community members been informed?
- In what ways has this chapter provided you with useful tools in implementing CCSS?

_____

_____

_____

_____

DIALOGIC ACTIVITY

Discuss with your colleagues and respond to the following questions:

- In what ways might marginalized students, educators, and parents/community members experience barriers at your school?
- How might a student new to your school, who is from a marginalized group, experience your school's regard for people like her?
- What are your thoughts about MUSD's approach to change in meeting CCSS?
- How did the phrase _fill-in-the-blank programs_ resonate with changes you have experienced as an educator?
- Please describe the mechanisms at your school to support marginalized students, educators, and parents/community members?
- What steps might you and your colleagues take to more closely examine the concepts of identity and belief systems in your environment?
- In what ways might the nested levels of commitment impact the English language and math programs in your district or school?

_____

_____

_____

_____

_____

_____

_____

_____

Having read to this point, you now have a solid understanding of important concepts—equity and inequity, a historical perspective on school reform efforts, and the Tools of Cultural Proficiency. With the next chapter, you begin an in-depth consideration of the promise of the Common Core State Standards. As a student of socially just educational practices, you will be equipped to approach the Common Core to ensure equity for your students.

4 Promise of the Common Core

If the Common Core promise is to be fulfilled, all educators and education stakeholders must commit to excellence and equity, because excellence cannot be achieved without equity.

—The Regional Equity Assistance Centers, 2013, p. 9

GETTING CENTERED

How do you define excellence for students, for educators? What is your definition of equity? What are some of the challenges and opportunities to bring excellence and equity together? In what ways might the Common Core address the equity gaps that currently exist?

_____

_____

_____

_____

EXAMINING THE PROMISE OF THE COMMON CORE STANDARDS

The purpose of this chapter is to identify ways in which educators can use the lens of Cultural Proficiency along with Common Core expectations to increase student and educator opportunities to learn and improve teaching and learning for all students. While some schools and districts have made progress in narrowing achievement gaps and preparing more students for success after high school, we know that we still have much to do to make college and career readiness real for every student. For example, a new Civil Rights Data Collection report compiled from data from all 97,000 of the nation's public schools, representing 49 million students, shows that access to college courses necessary for college is inequitably distributed.

> *Eighty-one percent of Asian-American high school students and 71 percent of white high school students attend high schools where the full range of math and science courses are offered (Algebra I, geometry, Algebra II, calculus, biology, chemistry, physics). However, fewer than half of American Indian and Native-Alaskan high school students have access to the full range of math and science courses in their high schools. Black students (57 percent), Latino students (67 percent), students with disabilities (63 percent), and English learner students (65 percent) also have diminished access to the full range of courses.* (Lhamon, 2014)

Along with poorer access to advanced coursework, data also show that many of these students may also be attending "majority-minority" schools with deficits in the availability of highly qualified teachers, high-quality curriculum, and personal attention to students (Darling-Hammond, 2007). Taken together, this illustrates that traditionally underrepresented and underserved students are, again, left out of strongly supported opportunities for graduation and advancement beyond. Early in 2010, President Obama refreshed the vision of an excellent education for all students.

> *We must do better. Together, we must achieve a new goal, that by 2020, the United States will once again lead the world in college completion. We must raise the expectations for our students, for our schools, and for ourselves—this must be a national priority. We must ensure that every student graduates from high school well prepared for college and a career. . . . This effort will require the skills and talents of many, but especially our nation's teachers, principals, and other school leaders. Our goal must be to have a great teacher in every classroom and a great principal in every school.* (U.S. Department of Education, 2010, paras. 3, 5)

Later that year, national and state leaders initiated the call to implement the Common Core State Standards (CCSS) as the pathway to educate all students with an eye beyond high school. Very quickly, most states and the District of Columbia adopted the standards or close adaptations and have since been focused on start-up activities, including teacher professional development, lesson planning, material selection, and understanding new, technology-based assessments. Now, that states and districts are engaged in the hard work of implementation, educators and stakeholders are beginning to ask if and how these efforts will impact student achievement results. How are CCSS leading to different results from initiatives, such as No Child Left Behind or the earlier Elementary and Secondary Education Act, that also promised a quality education for all students? How do we leverage expectations in CCSS into outcomes where every student graduates ready to capitalize on advanced learning and successful careers?

As we noted earlier, the purpose of this book is to explore how addressing CCSS can lead to more equitable results for students by leveraging effective leadership and ongoing professional learning, along with the Essential Elements of Cultural Proficiency and other tools. To begin this journey, it is necessary to understand what the CCSS are and are not through a brief overview of Common Core expectations, opportunities, challenges, and necessary shifts in mindsets and practices.

THE COMMON CORE

The CCSS initiative is the most recent effort of educators and policymakers to identify and organize what our American students should know and be able to do by Grade 12 to graduate immediately ready for success in college and careers. Reflecting on earlier standards-based reforms, state leaders agreed on the importance of fewer, higher, clearer standards for all students and established benchmarks for student learning in math and reading. Designers explain that the Common Core State Standards represent a coherent progression of learning expectations in English language arts and mathematics that define the knowledge and skills students should develop and master in their K–12 education. As a whole, the CCSS emphasize learning goals, describe end-of-year expectations, and focus on results, leaving room for principals and teachers to determine how these learning goals should be achieved.

ENGLISH LANGUAGE ARTS (ELA)

ELA standards include: (1) a comprehensive K–5 section, with Reading, Writing, Speaking and Listening, and Language strands; (2) a content-area-specific section for Grades 6–12 ELA, with Reading, Writing, Speaking and Listening, and Language strands; and (3) a content-area-specific section for Grades 6–12 history/social studies, science, and technical subjects, focused on Reading and Writing. Each strand includes a strand-specific set of broad College and Career Readiness (CCR) anchor standards. Individual grade-level standards are defined in K–8 and provide specificity; in Grades 9–12, the standards use two-year bands to provide flexibility for local educators in high school course design. Together the standards define the skills and understandings that all students must demonstrate.

Key Features of the ELA Standards. The Key Features describe important concepts within the ELA standards. These are the foundations for lesson and unit design and instructional stances that can include attention to student interests and needs, educator skills, and local context.

- **Reading:** Text complexity and growth of comprehension.
  - o The Reading standards place equal emphasis on the sophistication of what students read and the skill with which they read.
- **Writing:** Text types, responding to reading, and research.
  - o The Writing standards acknowledge the fact that some writing skills, such as the ability to plan, revise, edit, and publish, are applicable to many types of writing, while other skills are a better fit with specific writing types—arguments, informative or explanatory texts, and narratives.
- **Speaking and Listening:** Flexible communication and collaboration.
  - o The Speaking and Listening standards require students to develop a range of broadly useful oral communication and interpersonal skills, including, but not limited to, skills necessary for formal presentations.
- **Language:** Conventions, effective use, and vocabulary.
  - o The Language standards include the essential rules of standard written and spoken English, but acknowledge that using language allows an informed choice among alternatives.

The ELA standards do have content requirements—classic myths and stories, America's founding documents, foundational American literature, and Shakespeare. Also, the CCSS require that students learn about literature and other disciplines through reading, writing, speaking, and listening. States and local education agencies determine other subject matter requirements. This demonstrates that CCSS are not, themselves, a curriculum, nor do they prescribe a specific curriculum.

REFLECTION

Review the concepts in the Key Features and, also, the required content for ELA. Think about how you might address these when developing new learning assignments for struggling students or students from underrepresented demographic groups. In what ways might you work with your colleagues to design professional learning to meet these student needs?

_____

_____

_____

_____

MATHEMATICS

CCSS include Standards for Mathematical Practice and Standards for Mathematical Content. Let's first examine the standards for the focus on mathematical practice.

Standards for Mathematical Practice. The eight K–12 standards describe ways in which students should engage with the content, processes, and proficiencies of "longstanding importance" in mathematics. Students (1) make sense of problems and persevere in solving them; (2) reason abstractly and quantitatively; (3) construct viable arguments and critique the reasoning of others; (4) model with mathematics; (5) use appropriate tools strategically; (6) attend to precision; (7) look for and make use of structure; and (8) look for and express regularity in repeated reasoning. In Grades K–5, the standards provide a solid foundation in whole numbers, addition, subtraction, multiplication, division, fractions, and decimals. In Grades 6–8, a major emphasis is placed on the study of ratios, proportions, and algebra. In Grades 9–12, the standards require students to apply mathematical thinking to real-world problems. The CCSS require deep comprehension and the ability to apply mathematics to problems students have not encountered previously.

Now let's take a look at how the standards address mathematical content.

Standards for Mathematical Content. The standards for mathematical content are designed as learning progressions through the grades and define what students should understand and be able to do in mathematics. For kindergarten through Grade 8, there are grade-specific standards. At the high school level, the standards are organized by "conceptual categories." Each of these sets of standards includes a number of "domains," which group related standards to provide coherence around key mathematical ideas.

Grades K–8. There are grade-specific standards. Each contains a number of domains, including: (1) Counting and Cardinality; (2) Operations and Algebraic Thinking; (3) Number and Operations in Base Ten; (4) Fractions; (5) Ratios and Proportional Reasoning; (6) The Number System; (7) Expressions and Equations; (8) Functions; (9) Measurement and Data; (10) Geometry; and (11) Statistics and Probability.

Grades 9–12. The standards at the high school level outline the mathematics expected of all students in order to be prepared for college and a career. Also, they include additional mathematics for students who choose to take advanced-level courses. The high school standards are organized by "conceptual categories," each providing a "coherent view of high school mathematics." These include (1) Number and Quantity; (2) Algebra; (3) Functions; (4) Modeling; (5) Geometry; and (6) Statistics and Probability.

The standards and limited number of requirements in both ELA and mathematics offer room for educators to develop learning opportunities that address diverse student cultures and include differentiated options for a wide range of learners' interests and needs. Meshing the expectations of CCSS's academic rigor together with culturally responsive instruction builds equitable access, opportunities, and outcomes for all students. Later in this chapter, we will continue to explore this idea.

REFLECTION

Review the concepts in the Standards for Mathematical Practice and the Standards for Mathematical Content. Think about how you might address these when developing new learning assignments for struggling students or students from underrepresented demographic groups. What are a few of your ideas? In what ways might you and your colleagues design professional learning strategies to support educators in meeting these student needs?

SHIFTS IN TEACHING AND LEARNING

The Common Core State Standards, along with other newly developed expectations such as those in the Next Generation Science Standards (NGSS) and 21st century skills, point to a significant shift in education toward a deeper approach to learning—an approach that focuses on building both conceptual understanding and the language skills necessary to convey that understanding. States, districts, regional support providers, and others are drawing together patterns found across the

Common Core to help educators better understand these ELA and mathematics shifts.

Shifts in ELA. In a large conference for state and district educators, researchers, and private support providers, Student Achievement Partners summarized *major shifts* in ELA standards:

- Teachers help students build increasingly complex academic vocabulary.
- Teachers provide time and support for close reading of challenging text.
- Students read as much nonfiction as fiction.
- Students learn from fiction and nonfiction by reading, not by being told about the text.
- Students use evidence from text to make points during discussion of readings.
- Students use evidence to support points in expository or persuasive writing (Hulce, Hoehn, O'Day, & Walcott, 2013).

Shifts in Mathematics. At that same conference, Phil Daro, one of the Common Core mathematics panelists and long-time math educator and policy leader, summarized mathematics changes for educators and students:

- Educators ensure that skills are taught coherently within and across grades.
- Educators ensure that students deeply understand and can operate easily within a mathematics concept before moving on.
- Students learn more deeply about fewer key topics.
- Students develop fluency—that is, speed with accuracy—in performing simple calculations.
- Students can use mathematics and choose the appropriate concept for application without teacher prompting.
- Students are able both to think fast and to solve problems (Hulce et al., 2013).

REFLECTION

Think about the ELA and mathematics content summarized above and examine some of the required changes in teacher and student practice. Now, consider where your school is in addressing these CCSS expectations. What information did you use in making your assessment? What is your next step and what do you need to do—alone or with colleagues—to take that next step?

_____

_____

_____

_____

MAKING THE SHIFTS THAT COUNT

Making any of the changes inherent in successfully using the Common Core to increase every student's achievement and well-being necessitates a unified commitment to action among educators, policymakers, and stakeholders. Although 43 states and the District of Columbia have adopted the standards, for some, they are still quite controversial. Advocates say the CCSS are necessary to ensure that high school graduates are ready for college or career and that those against Common Core are politically motivated to disrupt the initiative. However, detractors claim the CCSS embody serious design flaws related to developmentally inappropriate learning progressions or demonstrate federal meddling in local authority, setting up a de facto national curriculum. Advocates for the Common Core counter that the standards are desired outcomes, not specified curriculum or instruction. They point to text in the CCSS documents themselves to make their case, for example, the Introduction to the CCSS for Mathematics, which states, "These Standards do not dictate curriculum or teaching methods" (p. 5) and the ELA Standards that make a similar point: "The Standards define what all students are expected to know and be able to do, not how teachers should teach" (p. 6). The debate about the pros and cons of the Common Core has led several states to rethink or modify their support for the standards, causing some to be confused about whether to move CCSS implementation forward or hold in place until all is settled.

COMMON CORE CHALLENGES

Educators moving ahead with new Common Core work will undoubtedly face a variety of challenges. Even simple changes can cause discomfort or uncertainty. The major shifts required in putting more complex curriculum directed toward every student's being ready for college and careers is not different. However, identifying which factors might be obstacles to implementation is the first step in active problem solving. Several areas of concern are being expressed by educators and policymakers and are described in many education reports, some of which are summarized below.

DIFFERENT RESULTS

How the Common Core affects struggling students is a question that can't be answered until the standards are fully implemented. Much will depend on how students are taught and supported. However, by looking again at the achievement patterns that developed under the No Child Left Behind (NCLB) Act, the previous federal initiative to reduce the achievement gap, we can get some idea of what to expect with the new standards, although the conclusions about NCLB successes or failures are varied (Clark & Cookson, 2012).

TEACHERS/TEACHING/INSTRUCTION

Without clear information about what the Common Core Standards require and without supports to ensure the implementation of rigorous expectations, teachers may struggle to adequately and equitably implement the standards (Almy, 2012; Clifford, 2014). If traditional strategies are implemented, underserved students will receive least prepared teachers.

> *English language learners have a right to appropriate education that is grounded in sound theory and implemented in ways that address their needs systematically, through coordinated support linking teachers, materials, formative assessments, tests and accountability systems, and technology.* (Kenji Hakuta and Maria Santos in the Regional Equity Assistance Centers, 2013, p. 9)

STUDENT ACCESS

Having rigorous standards does not guarantee high-need students can access or master them. If students are not successful, new standards are meaningless. Failure to provide low-income, Latino, African American, and English-learning students access to high-quality, standards-based instruction will leave them even more unprepared for college and the workplace. Research and experience confirm that poor students and students of color are more likely than their more advantaged peers to receive low-level assignments (Education Trust-West, 2012).

CURRICULUM/CONTENT

Standards are guides, not the rigorous lessons and supports needed to teach.

Alone, the new standards will not bring us closer to becoming a nation of college- and career-ready students. The new standards lay out a rigorous framework describing the learning outcomes students should reach, but they do not provide any guidance on the content that should be used. The hard work of translating individual standards into a sequence of lessons that are actually meaningful and instructive to students is still to come. (Almy, 2012 p. 2)

RESOURCES—TIME

Replacing lectures with interactive learning and meeting higher expectations for deeper learning requires more classroom time. Figuring out structures to provide extra instructional time for individual and groups of students, while supporting student participation in nonacademic activities, is significant (Farbman, Goldberg, & Miller, 2014).

For professional development activities to be productive, they must be priorities and must be given consistent and uninterrupted blocks of time that are protected and separate for regular classroom instructional activities. Addressing professional learning for teachers and administrators with so many emerging expectations already puts strains on limited time and financial resources (Clifford & Mason, 2013; Farbman et al., 2014).

REFLECTION

As you move ahead on the Common Core implementation, what challenges are you currently facing? What additional challenges are you anticipating? How prepared do you feel to tackle them? What might you need to increase your skills or confidence to be successful?

_____

_____

_____

_____

COMMON CORE OPPORTUNITIES

According to a study sponsored by the Council of Chief State School Officers, the Common Core has the potential to help schools elevate the academic performance of all students while also addressing the pervasive gaps that separate students (EdTrust-West, 2012). The CCSS development teams used a number of sources, including the frameworks for the OECD (Organisation for Economic Co-operation and Development) Program for International Student Assessment and Trends in International Mathematics and Science Study; the International Baccalaureate syllabi; reports by American Institutes for Research; standards from high-performing countries; and research conducted by Achieve, ACT, and the College Board (e.g., *Ready or Not: Creating a High School Diploma That Counts* by Achieve) to make this assertion (EdTrust-West, 2012). However, as educators are in planning and early implementation modes, they are seeing how to "flip the switch" themselves to look at the opportunities within the new challenges. For example, an impromptu, after-meeting group continued to discuss the Common Core and their desire to "take back control" of how new practices would look at their schools. The group of K–12 school and district educators listed potential opportunities gleaned from earlier conversations and professional reading. Possibilities they listed included:

- New courses to meet CCSS means opportunity to remove timeworn prerequisites that serve as filters or barriers to advanced courses.
- The call for "personalization"—should move more teachers to link academics with problems and materials of interest to students.
- Student-generated, project-based learning should provide more room for a range of student responses that are unique and reflect cultural and linguistic variations.
- The expectation for "deep learning" means that students will have more time on a topic or lesson instead of leapfrogging to a new topic—should be helpful to students needing more time to engage with content.
- The expectation that "academic language" or vocabulary will be part of every teacher's process—should be helpful to English language learners, for example.
- Common learning processes, such as problem identification and hypotheses are applied in English Language Arts, Mathematics, and Sciences—the alignment should help students have multiple opportunities to learn and practice these strategies.
- New ways of teaching and learning support the opportunity to reframe educators' and students' ideas and attitudes about intelligence—known as a "growth" mindset, that is, perceiving intelligence and skills as innate or "fixed," as opposed to things that can be improved through effort and experience.

- Establishing new educator networks, including teachers who have unique assignments, because teachers across districts and states are working on Common Core Standards and can share what works in ways that have not previously been possible.

The challenges and opportunities that are part of implementing the CCSS center on how best to address the needs of all students, especially those who have been traditionally underserved and underrepresented. Hamilton and Mackinnon (2013) describe a design opportunity for high schools that acknowledges thoughts of policymakers, researchers, and K–12 educators in the field:

> *The key lesson of all this work is that schools are the place where the Common Core will or will not make a transformative difference in the learning of American students, particularly those who have struggled to reach high levels of learning under existing systems. To realize the full power of the Common Core, we must look to... schools and reshape them to support teachers and maximize key resources, rather than implement partial solutions that are likely to result in weak performance or even failure.* (p. 7)

As CCSS implementation continues, it is very clear that it is educators who must be able to execute Common Core potential by transforming challenges into opportunities. For example, they must move *from* deterring students from or "dumbing down" gatekeeper courses such as algebra *to* rethinking algebra instruction to provide more innovative learning opportunities that inspire and motivate students to persist, along with alternative learning supports for struggling students.

CCSS EXPECT MORE FROM EVERYONE

While the CCSS have generated debates and challenges, along with the potential for making a big difference in the lives of students, the purpose of this book is not to arbitrate various controversies nor tout as yet unproven strategies. Rather, our perspective is that most states have adopted the Common Core, want to implement it well, and look forward to improving student learning results.

By consensus, most agree that the CCSS define the knowledge and skills students need to succeed in college and careers and increase our expectations to the level of other high-performing countries. The standards are considered a "higher bar" for student performance, meaning a higher bar for educators, support providers, schools, and districts. Everyone has to make changes in approaches to teaching and learning.

The CCSS, then, highlight outcomes for students and embed expectations for teachers, principals, and other staff. The content standards with performance expectations guided by new assessments identify *what* students should know and be able to do and by when. This informs the priority work of teachers—*what* teachers are to know and be able to do to ensure all students experience effective instruction and support to meet grade-level goals and thrive. What teachers need to develop their individual and collective capacity to continuously improve practice and results frames *what* principals need to know and be able to do. The job of principals, then, is to guide, support, and monitor teaching and learning that leads to continuously improving student and staff growth and well-being, resulting in graduation and future success for every student.

AN IMPORTANT POINT OF CLARIFICATION

To be clear, when the authors use the phrases "implementing the Common Core" or "CCSS implementation," we are not suggesting rote installation of the standards—quite the contrary. Our assumption throughout the book is that educators will thoughtfully consider the standards in light of the needs and assets of their students, taking special care to address student populations who have been least successful in ELA and mathematics achievement, and who continue to be underrepresented and underserved in rigorous academics and sustained assistance. While the CCSS organize content and require stronger instruction and support, the new standards may still be missing the point for underserved and underrepresented students.

For educators to transform their effectiveness in using appropriate, differentiated approaches to teaching and learning, we believe that fusing Common Core expectations with the lens of Cultural Proficiency is critical. The set of concepts, school stories, frameworks, and tools in this book offer educators resources to use in implementing CCSS in their schools, districts, and states so that all students, including those traditionally underserved, graduate on time, ready for success in advanced education and fulfilling careers.

GOING DEEPER

The title of this chapter indicates the *promise* of the Common Core. Go back and read some of your earlier reflections in this chapter. Where are you with your commitment to the Common Core? What do you understand to be the promise of the Common Core? To what extent do you embrace the Common Core as a vehicle for extending the promise of access and equity to your students?

_____

_____

_____

_____

DIALOGIC ACTIVITY

You and your colleagues have had the opportunity to review and, in some cases, to engage in new learning in this chapter. In what ways does this chapter inform your continued professional learning? What new questions surface for your group as you anticipate professional learning related to the Common Core over the next few years? What specific recommendations can you make to school leaders to inform them of your desires and needs?

_____

_____

_____

_____

Now that we addressed the promise and the challenges of the Common Core Standards, let's take a look at how leaders can intentionally and mindfully use the lens of Culturally Proficient Professional Learning to implement the Common Core Standards in ways to ensure equitable outcomes for all students. Chapter 5 presents the role of school leaders as instrumental in planning and implementing quality professional learning that is aligned with continuous improvement for teachers and students with a focus on equity and access.

5 Leadership and the Common Core

The effective change leader actively participates as a learner in helping the organization improve.

—Michael Fullan, 2011, p. 5

GETTING CENTERED

Michael Fullan is recognized as a worldwide authority on organizational change, both from the perspectives of theory and practice. He is a strong advocate of leaders who first research "best practices," especially those in difficult circumstances; who then try out those new ideas, collect data, and draw conclusions about those practices from the data; and who, finally, expand on those practices and continue to collect data on the new practices. This effective, intentional, mindful leader is involved as an active learner, sustaining the learning from the regular practice (Fullan, 2013). How does Fullan's description of leadership align with the leadership at your school and district? In what ways do you lead? When was the last time you really changed the way you teach or lead? What happened to help you make that change?

_____

_____

_____

_____

THE PRINCIPAL'S ROLE IN IMPLEMENTING THE COMMON CORE

The purpose of this chapter is to examine the role of school leaders as they design and implement the Common Core State Standards (CCSS) through high-quality professional development/learning. We will emphasize the need for improving practice through professional development as an opportunity to improve student outcomes as intended by the CCSS.

The role of building principals has been evolving over time to become more focused on instructional leadership, and that role has never been more important than in this new age of CCSS and teacher effectiveness.

> *To date we have not found a single case of a school improving its student achievement record in the absence of talented leadership.* (Louis, Leithwood, Wahlstrom, & Anderson, 2010, p. 11)

This quote comes from the findings of a comprehensive study by Karen Seashore Louis and her colleagues that identify areas of leadership that most strongly connect with student achievement.

As the quote attests, research is confirming what common sense has told us for years—effective leadership plays an important role in making effective schools that ensure each and every child achieves. A sample of three studies makes this point. Research has shown the effect of leadership on student learning as second only to classroom instruction (Leithwood, Louis, Anderson, & Wahlstrom, 2004). And, important to our purpose of educating all students to high standards, there are studies, such as a middle school study in California, finding that effective school leaders have the largest impact on schools with the greatest need (Williams, Kirst, & Haertel, 2010). Also, *district* leadership has been found to have a positive influence on turning around low-performing schools (Honig, Copland, Rainey, Lorton, & Newton, 2010). Conclusion: effective leadership matters. It always has.

REFLECTION

What is *your* thinking about why leadership is so important to school improvement and student achievement? Which leadership functions and/or behaviors that you noted do you believe will be most important in fulfilling the potential of the Common Core?

_____

_____

_____

_____

IMPLEMENTING THE COMMON CORE

Moving Common Core concepts from paper to practice requires effective leaders, teachers, and staff working together and with families and the community on behalf of students. No matter how well written the CCSS policy, its ultimate effect depends on principals' implementing the change through individual or collective leadership. Fixsen and Blase (2009) identify implementation as the "missing link" in the successful translation of evidence-based theories and models to practice.

> *It is not enough to identify advanced standards, high quality instructional materials, and effective instructional practices; school communities must be able to successfully establish and integrate multiple program components and sustain effective instructional practices in order to ensure high-quality teaching and learning experiences for all students.* (p. 1)

Principals and district leaders are expected to execute a full-court press to implement the CCSS. Successful implementation requires principals to collaborate with teachers and staff to develop the standards into a working curriculum where teacher capacity matches up with student needs and school resources. This process can mean transforming instruction by using new assessments, initiating new educator evaluation, and organizing support systems (Canole & Young, 2013). To enact these shifts, the leader must know and be able to use sound principles and processes, weigh contextual factors, reshape structural elements when needed, and then carry out specific interventions or innovations (Fixen & Blase, 2009). While challenging, considering these multiple variables in combination rather than one at a time yields better overall results (The Wallace Foundation, 2013). Skillful principals can be effective in leading these changes because they are able to discriminate between challenges that are adaptive, such as trying to change mindsets, from those that are technical, such as selecting and executing the appropriate solution, and moving on them differently (Fixen, Blase, Horner, Sims, & Sugai, 2013).

The leader's ability to identify different situations and anticipate or respond appropriately is especially important in implementing rigorous, standards-based programs that educate and support students with varied cultures, socioeconomic status, ethnicities, races, languages, special needs, sexual orientations, and other demographics most challenged by the status quo.

REFLECTION

The research summarized in the previous section is telling us that implementing multiple changes at the same time can actually produce better results than approaching them one at a time. Why do you think this might be true? This finding might suggest a shift in our expectations for principals—*from* someone with the ability to maintain a singular focus until task completion *to* someone who can take on several tasks simultaneously. From your experience, what are the pros and cons of each perspective?

_____

_____

_____

_____

RETHINKING THE PRINCIPAL'S ROLE

Leadership demands, such as those inherent in the Common Core, are asking us to reconsider how we think about the work of principals and other school leaders. While the role of the principal has been changing for the past two decades or more, new CCSS expectations make it clear that principals are, first, instructional leaders who must make sure that that each child is college and career ready upon graduation from high school and that each teacher effectively meets the diverse learning needs of his or her students on a daily basis. For this to happen, the principal must employ the practice of continuous school improvement and support. This strategy guides teachers to steadily increase their academic and instructional capacity to address Common Core outcomes by ensuring high levels of student learning, inclusive of students who, traditionally, have been underserved.

REFLECTION

How long have you been an education leader? What have been your roles as leader? Over that time, how have expectations for what you do and the scope and intensity of your role changed? How easy or hard was it for you to make the shift? Using this experience when you are leading Common Core changes may give you an insight into how others handle change.

_____

_____

_____

_____

LEADERSHIP AND STUDENT ACHIEVEMENT

Effective leadership means that educators take actions that result in improving school effectiveness and increasing teacher performance and student learning results. Policy standards, the Interstate School Leadership Licensure Standards (ISLLC; Council of Chief State School Officers, 2008), serve as de facto national standards that describe leadership functions shown by research and professional literature to be most important to the work of principals and other leaders. A companion document, *Performance Expectations and Indicators for Education Leaders* (Sanders & Kearney, 2008), describes observable leader behaviors. Together, these present what education leaders should know and be able to do to be licensed and in practice.

The strongest link between effective leadership and student learning results is reported in two large, comprehensive studies (Leithwood et al., 2004; Louis et al., 2010) that align with the core concept of the ISLLC leadership standards. The findings identify five leadership areas with the strongest link between leadership and student achievement. With student achievement as a key outcome of CCSS, and the press of many changes under way, these elements have direct import for those leading Common Core implementation efforts. Research indicates that school leaders can have especially strong impact in the following areas:

- **Setting Direction**

  To ensure successful implementation of the CCSS at the school level, principals must set the tone for the importance of the emerging changes, even though they may be challenging. The success of Common Core implementation hinges on principals clearly prioritizing the standards as the basis for instruction and professional learning. Leaders can ensure that a key objective for the school community is to establish—and act on—high expectations for all staff and students, including those most in need of extra help. Schools with principals demonstrating a strong vision are more likely to successfully enact reform efforts and achieve higher performance scores.

- **Developing People**

Districts that are serious about high-quality Common Core implementation select, evaluate, and hold principals accountable based on their skills in instruction. Administrators need not shoulder the responsibility of leadership alone. Leadership can be shared with master teachers, instructional coaches, or others. Effective principals deliberately plan and implement progressive leadership opportunities for teacher development.

School leaders play a crucial role in building teacher capacity and increasing teacher effectiveness. Leaders help build teacher capacity by providing specific opportunities and supports for teachers to extend their knowledge and skills to address the needs of all students. Principals support different examples of professional learning, for example, individual coaching, direct feedback, addressing equity challenges in learning communities, grade- or subject-level collaboration around student work, or practicing new teaching and assessment models. The principal collaborates with staff in developing individual professional growth plans that identify specific objectives for individual or collective learning connected to helping students reach CCSS expectations. The plan also connects professional learning to a fair and rigorous evaluation system, using multiple types of data as evidence of performance and accomplishment.

- **Managing the Instructional Program**

Principals work with teachers and support staff to ensure that the instructional system addresses students' assets and needs, while also meeting expectations of the school community, and state and federal requirements.

Being instructional leaders now means, for example, that principals have the skills to introduce the new standards and identify schoolwide professional learning needs. They are able to support individual teachers and groups of teachers in designing curriculum and aligned formative assessments. Principals conduct formal and informal evaluations and provide useful feedback to staff. They collect student data and analyze results of disaggregated information looking for disparities indicating inequitable practices.

- **Fostering Collaboration**

  When teachers collectively engage in participatory decision-making, designing lessons, using data, and examining student work, they are able to deliver rigorous and relevant learning for all students and personalize learning for individual students. Principals ensure that teachers do not work in isolation from one another, but, instead, work collaboratively, giving each other help and guidance to improve instructional practices. This may require restructuring the school schedule to provide staff with dedicated time to work collaboratively to learn new strategies for academic instruction, use a cultural proficiency lens to assess current practices, or solve learning challenges their students face. The leader may pull together teachers and staff to work on curriculum development or new student behavior interventions and supports. Peer learning among small groups of teachers is the most powerful predictor of improved student achievement over time (Berry, Daughtrey, & Wieder, 2009).

- **Shaping Organizational Structure and Culture**

  A principal's actions establish workplace conditions that allow teachers and staff to fully apply their knowledge and skills. School leaders work with others to diagnose the school's capacity and environment, develop and implement action plans, and manage time and resources in support of school goals. Because the school's culture and climate can shape what teachers and students can and cannot do, effective principals handle planning and operations efficiently while also building a culture of schoolwide collaboration, equity, and shared accountability. They know that teachers with positive working environments are more satisfied and plan to stay longer in their schools. In addition, their students make more academic progress than similar students in schools with poor working conditions (Johnson, Kraft, & Papay, 2012).

SHARED LEADERSHIP

Shared leadership is referenced in the descriptions of Karen Louis's leadership areas (Louis et al., 2010). Distributing leadership to teachers and staff (along with communities and students, when appropriate) is a critical factor in enacting CCSS. Sharing leadership makes it more possible to meet our moral responsibility to reach every student with differentiated support. Not only is distributing leadership to staff important, so is distributing responsibility for continuous professional improvement and accountability for growth, performance, and results. Distributed leadership can have a positive impact on the quality of our schools, with teachers, school staff, and district office staff working together to ensure student learning and well-being. To scale up school improvements, districts and schools need to build overall capacity *and* specialized skills. This expanded capacity is not possible if control is limited to a few individuals—it requires a broader distribution of leadership (Elmore, 2000).

By attending to Louis's five impact areas, individually or collectively with shared leadership teams, principals increase the likelihood that their leadership will contribute to increased student achievement. While there are many measures of student and educator success, those who have adopted the Common Core have student graduation and readiness for advanced learning in college and careers as their markers of accomplishment. How confident are current principals and other leaders that they are prepared to lead?

READINESS TO LEAD THE COMMON CORE

Principals, like teachers, need professional learning and support to make the most of the Common Core. What are principals saying they need to do a good job? A 2013 report by researchers Matthew Clifford and Christine Mason presents results from a survey of more than 1,000 principals from 14 states. A sample of results includes the following:

- While most districts and schools have already begun implementing CCSS, principals believed that they were underprepared for full implementation, particularly in programs for special population students and expanded learning opportunities (p. 13).
- Principals indicated that they felt prepared to *initiate* change efforts by convening and motivating staff members, but are learning to lead improvements on their own without specific professional development targeted to leadership tasks (p. 16).
- Principals believed they had "set the stage" for Common Core, but they were less sure about how to proceed with incorporating changes in curriculum and instruction into day-to-day activities in schools (p. 16).
- For Common Core implementation success, principals must create conditions for the integration of standards into practice, with fidelity.

However, principals didn't have full information on costs, strategies, or monitoring approaches because few of them had professional development on leadership processes (p. 17).

- Principals reported that they had not incorporated the Common Core into teacher evaluations; not related CCSS to instructional strategies for specific student populations; not used the new standards in expanded learning opportunities (extended day, afterschool, or summer programs) to support CCSS (p.17).

Results from the Clifford and Mason study highlight principals' leadership gaps related to the Common Core. Principals not only need additional information about CCSS expectations and content, they also require specific instructional training that they need in supervising teachers and providing meaningful feedback. These leaders lack confidence in integrating processes such as teacher evaluation with CCSS, but will most likely be evaluated, themselves, against that expectation. Finally, principals are not holding students from diverse demographic groups to the higher core standards, nor are they using proven strategies that these students need to learn, catch up, and successfully reach Common Core outcomes. Education leaders need to seize the professional learning opportunities that are part of the initial rollouts and also advocate for leader-oriented support. Moreover, these principals can morph the challenge of designing CCSS curriculum that is appropriate for diverse student populations into an opportunity that engages cultural proficiency tools in the development of new, rigorous lessons that are accessible and interesting to students.

The fusion of Common Core expectations with the lens of Culturally Proficient leadership is a new way of approaching curriculum and instruction, leadership, and professional learning—just as CCSS is a new approach to academic learning for a broader group of students. Some leaders have been working in this way for a long time; for other leaders, there remain serious doubts that many students can meet Common Core goals. George Theoharis (2007) reports in his study that principals *who came to the field with a calling to do social justice work* (p. 222) were able to raise student achievement, improve school structures, build staff capacity, and strengthen school culture and community—elements that reflect Louis's and colleagues' leadership and student achievement connection.

So, to lead this new work, education leaders must check up on their own assumptions and beliefs about who can learn high-level content and discuss it with sophisticated, academic, analytic, and evidence-based language. And, as we will see in the next section, principals must consider how quality professional learning, with the lens of Cultural Proficiency, strengthens the likelihood that effective CCSS implementation leads to college- and career-ready graduates.

REFLECTION

Take a minute to reflect on your own assumptions and beliefs about who can and will not likely succeed in graduating ready for college and careers. Examine the ways in which your leadership is part of the problem (systemic inequities) or part of the solution (equitable leadership).

_____

_____

_____

_____

COMMON CORE AND PROFESSIONAL LEARNING

As you begin this section, think about your current conception of professional development. How do you distinguish the terms growth and progress from improvement, achievement, and success? From your perspective, how are these being used in our transition to the Common Core, and what are the implications for students and educators?

_____

_____

_____

_____

Earlier in the book we identified emerging changes in teaching and learning because of rigorous CCSS expectations. Common Core implementation requires educators and leaders to have deep understanding of the standards and instructional skills needed to address a wide range of diverse students striving to graduate college and career ready. Educators must not only *know* what is needed, they must be able to *do* what is needed to make the shifts in schools and classroom practice. Therefore, professional learning for CCSS centers on adult learning approaches that ultimately, help *all* students reach the standards.

FROM PROFESSIONAL DEVELOPMENT TO PROFESSIONAL LEARNING

Thinking about the changes required for teachers, principals, and other educators sets the context for the why, what, and how of professional learning. New requirements and expectations for teaching and leading establish a new frame for professional learning and what makes it effective.

According to Learning Forward, the national professional learning organization formerly known as the National Council of Staff Development, "The decision to call these Standards for Professional *Learning* rather than Standards for Professional *Development* signals the importance of educators taking an active role in their continuous improvement and places emphasis on the learning" (Learning Forward, 2011, p. 13). This is because the [professional learning] standards call for a new form of educator learning that reflects what teachers and leaders need to know and be able to do to meet the academic and support needs of their students. Lois Brown Easton contends, "'Developing' is not enough. Educators must be knowledgeable and wise. They must know enough in order to change. They must change in order to get different results. They must become learners, and they must be self-developing (2008, p. 756). She, like other researchers, suggests that the most powerful learning occurs through active learning opportunities embedded in teachers' work—starting with teachers' assessments of what students need, followed by what teachers identify as areas for their own learning. As Sherri Leo and Jane Coggshall note, "Professional learning for teachers is moving out of the professional development workshop approach and into more authentic settings" (2013, p. 5).

STUDENTS AT THE CENTER OF EDUCATOR LEARNING

It is becoming very clear that educators must continuously improve to be smart enough and skilled enough to meet the learning needs of all students. What makes efforts to train and support teachers in the Common Core so important are that the effects of the standards on student learning depend entirely on teachers' ability to improve instruction and support to help students achieve. Author Doug Lemov emphasizes, "Strategies that do not develop the overall level of teacher skill merely determine who gets access to the scarce and precious resource of high-quality teaching" (2013, p. 53). That makes equity issues, such as student access to rigorous content and an effective teacher, part of the DNA of quality professional development. As discussed earlier, there can be no excellence without equity.

CCSS expectations of what students must know and be able to do to graduate ready for college and careers are clearly stated for educators. Simply put, then, educators must know the content as well and learn to help all students meet their goals. For example, looking into the English Language Arts standards, we see that students have specific learning expectations for reading and also for writing and speaking. This means that teachers must not only know and understand the grade-level content, but also know how and with what materials to instruct diverse students in learning how to conduct close reading of complex texts or to communicate their thinking through speaking or writing. The example highlights one of Learning Forward's key principles for quality professional learning: "Educators' commitment to students, all students, is the foundation of effective professional learning" (2011, p. 15). A comprehensive study of professional learning by Learning Forward and Stanford University concurred, when noting that well-designed, research-based professional learning can be a primary lever for improved educator practice and student results when it is rooted in student and educator needs (Wei et al., 2010). These expectations for student learning and instruction necessitate robust professional learning experiences and support systems for teachers and also principals.

REFLECTION

When we work in the field of education, we commit to the journey of life-long learning. Along this journey we are constantly faced with hurdles of change. As our society evolves, we find ourselves adjusting our educational practice to meet these demanding needs in the midst of change. The Common Core is providing educators with another opportunity to be learners as we adjust our mindset to match the expectations set by this new initiative. (Brennan, 2014, p. 2)

Celina Brennan's blog posting presents professional learning as an opportunity to "adjust our mindset." After reading her perspective, what are *you* thinking about the changes you should and/or will make? What implications might there be for increasing student access to CCSS courses or other goals of the Common Core?

_____

_____

_____

_____

AN OPPORTUNITY FOR NEW LEARNING

The end goals of the CCSS require a different type of teaching and learning for educators as well as students. As the majority of teachers around the country transition to the Common Core State Standards, designed to emphasize challenging concepts and skills, such as critical thinking, complexity, collaboration, and reasoning, many educators must deepen their practices. Common Core has implications for shifts in curriculum planning, differentiated instruction, materials and technology, and formative and summary assessments. Classroom dynamics are changing from teacher-led activities to shared responsibility among the teachers and students. Traditional professional development is no longer the right fit to meet the curriculum, assessment, instructional, and leadership changes the new standards demand.

It seems, then, that one of the most important things education leaders can do to help the Common Core initiative achieve the student outcomes is to support teachers in improving their practice. While designing and organizing new ways of educator learning may be another Common Core challenge, the new CCSS standards may also present opportunities. Teacher effectiveness expert and consultant, Charlotte Danielson, explains,

> *The Common Core rests on a view of teaching as complex decision making, as opposed to something more routine or drill-based. . . . It requires instructional strategies on teachers' parts that enable students to explore concepts and discuss them with each other, to question and respectfully challenge classmates' assertions. So I see the Common Core as a fertile and rich opportunity for really important professional learning by teachers, because—I don't know now how to say this nicely—well, not all teachers have been prepared to teach in this way.* (Rebora, 2013, p. 2)

To adequately prepare for the CCSS and the new testing that is rolling out, teachers and principals need rich, contextualized professional learning opportunities and regularly scheduled collaboration time. In suggesting approaches appropriate to educator learning, Leo and Coggshall (2013) include in-school professional learning communities, such as teacher lesson-study groups and just-in-time coaching support in classrooms. From their perspective, the transition from undifferentiated and decontextualized professional development to job-embedded professional learning could not come at a more opportune time as teachers work to understand and integrate the types of instruction targeted by the CCSS (Coggshall, 2012).

CHARACTERISTICS OF EFFECTIVE PROFESSIONAL LEARNING—RESEARCH

With the investment needed for educator professional learning—time, money, personnel, technology, and materials, for example—it makes sense to scan the literature for evidence-based characteristics of "good" professional learning. This information, combined with suggestions from those already weighing in on CCSS earlier in our work, together offer a rich set of characteristics for the content and adult learning strategies most likely to yield increased educator capacity to teach students well.

A very significant study on a range of professional learning questions was conducted in 2009 for the National Staff Development Council by Stanford University (Wei, Darling-Hammond, Andree, Richardson, & Orphanos, 2009). The study described that according to the research, high-quality professional-learning opportunities include the following seven characteristics. They are:

- Rooted in student and educator needs,
- Focused on content and pedagogy,
- Designed to ensure equitable outcomes,
- Ongoing, intensive, and embedded in practice,
- Collaborative, with an emphasis on shared accountability,
- Supported by adequate resources, and
- Coherent and aligned with other standards, policies, and programs.

These professional learning characteristics cut across disciplines, subject matter, grade levels, and educator career stages. As the Common Core is not a curriculum, these characteristics are not a program. They are drivers of effective adult learning. Working with these characteristics, educators can begin to shape individual and collective professional learning that research indicates is most effective *and* that addresses locally identified needs. The characteristics can also be useful in determining professional learning options from several selections.

In *High-Quality Professional Development for All Teachers: Effectively Allocating Resources*, Sarah Archibald presents a different list with some similarities (Archibald, 2011). From another perspective, they share that high-quality professional development does the following:

- Aligns with school goals, state and district standards and assessments, and other professional-learning activities.
- Focuses on core content and modeling of teaching strategies for the content.
- Includes opportunities for active learning of new teaching strategies.

- Provides the chance for teachers to collaborate.
- Includes follow-up and continuous feedback.

Together, these findings identify a set of characteristics that provides some direction and support for crafting professional learning opportunities that are likely to be more effective than others. There are many other studies and reports that probe aspects of professional learning planning, execution, and effect that could inform the lists. However, putting these characteristics into planning, practice, and program evaluation settings will press educators to look for or create a more detailed tool. National, state, and local *professional learning* standards further define effective professional learning programs and/or systems. Again, educators can make the final selection on which frame to use or if designing their own criteria, locally, works better for them.

REFLECTION

When you think about the professional development or professional learning you have experienced, what first comes to mind? Did you remember an engaging, productive, or frustrating time? Use information from the chapter to help you consider how you might extend or fix your experience in your next professional learning opportunity.

SHAPING PROFESSIONAL LEARNING—STANDARDS

Because educator continuous improvement is necessary to attain Common Core outcomes, effective and efficient professional learning is essential. Professional learning standards, built on reviews of evidence-based criteria and professional expertise, assist educators in finding and keeping on a pathway of steady improvement. The professional learning standards work together with student standards to push learning and growth toward Common Core outcomes. When used well, they also intersect with professional teaching and leadership standards to describe expectations for both program and personnel change. Professional learning standards guide educators, individually or collectively, into growth opportunities that are interesting and productive. Professional learning is a major lever in supporting and shifting instructional practice, ultimately leading to student learning and well-being.

STANDARDS FOR PROFESSIONAL LEARNING

Learning Forward is a national association squarely focused on professional learning.

Its online Overview (www.learningforward.org) details seven Professional Learning Standards that focus on educator effectiveness and results for all students. The Learning Forward Professional Learning Standards (2011) are:

Learning Communities

Occurs within learning communities committed to continuous improvement, collective responsibility, and goal alignment.

Leadership

Requires skillful leaders who develop capacity, advocate, and create support systems for professional learning.

Resources

Requires prioritizing, monitoring, and coordinating resources for educator learning.

Data

Uses a variety of sources and types of student, educator, and system data to plan, assess, and evaluate professional learning.

Learning Designs

Integrates theories, research, and models of human learning to achieve its intended outcomes.

Implementation

Applies research on change and sustains support for implementation of professional learning for long-term change.

Outcomes

Aligns its outcomes with educator performance and student curriculum standards.

The standards outline the characteristics of professional learning that lead to effective teaching practices, supportive leadership, and improved student results. The standards make explicit that the purpose of professional learning is for educators to develop the knowledge, skills, practices, and dispositions they need to help students perform at higher levels. The standards are not a prescription for how education leaders should address all the challenges related to improving the performance of educators and their students. Instead, the standards focus on one critical issue—professional learning.

The professional learning that occurs when these standards are fully implemented enrolls educators as active partners in determining the content of their learning, how their learning occurs, and how they evaluate its effectiveness.

The Overview for the Professional Learning standards indicates that "widespread attention to the standards increases equity of access to a high-quality education for every student, not just for those lucky enough to attend schools in more advantaged communities" (Learning Forward, 2011). Educators can use the standards to plan, facilitate, and evaluate professional learning that promises to heighten the quality of educator learning, performance of all educators, and student learning. These national standards have been adopted or adapted by states and districts.

THE SUPERINTENDENT'S QUALITY PROFESSIONAL LEARNING STANDARDS

This set of professional learning standards was approved by California's Superintendent of Public Instruction in December 2013 and has been rolling out across the state. The impetus for the new standards came from the state's Educator Excellence Task Force, which recommended a system of professional learning that brings together the goals of the state, districts, and schools, as well as individual educator needs. A focus throughout their report emphasized recognizing and addressing the unique assets and needs of California's diverse student population as a priority. Specifically, the report called for a focus on "students with disabilities; students from minority cultural, racial, and linguistic demographic groups; and students from low-income families" (California Department of Education & the Commission on Teacher Credentialing, 2012, p. 53). The report also stressed that quality professional learning must provide a continuum of opportunities for educators to learn and practice skills that advance expertise throughout their careers, from preparation through expert practice.

The seven Quality Professional Learning Standards (QPLS) represent essential components of a comprehensive, research-based, quality professional learning system that is appropriate for California, and we include them here for your consideration, as they might apply to your school or district. These standards include:

- **Data**—Quality professional learning uses varied sources and kinds of information to guide priorities, design, and assessments.
- **Content and Pedagogy**—Quality professional learning enhances educators' expertise to increase students' capacity to learn and thrive.
- **Equity**—Quality professional learning focuses on equitable access, opportunities, and outcomes for all students, with an emphasis on addressing achievement and opportunity disparities between student groups.
- **Design and Structure**—Quality professional learning reflects evidence-based approaches, recognizing that focused, sustained learning enables educators to acquire, implement, and assess improved practices.
- **Collaboration and Shared Accountability**—Quality professional learning facilitates the development of a shared purpose for student learning and collective responsibility for achieving it.
- **Resources**—Quality professional learning dedicates resources that are adequate, accessible, and allocated appropriately toward established priorities and outcomes.
- **Alignment and Coherence**—Quality professional learning contributes to a coherent system of educator learning and support that connects district, school, and individual priorities and needs with state and federal requirements and resources.

As the California state report recommended, equity, access, differentiated learning for educators and students, and attention to demographic, cultural, and physical individualities are embedded in each of the standards and featured in the Equity Standard. The QPLS also include brief narratives for each standard and more detailed elements and indicators that provide two additional levels that can be used at the policy level through specific career planning.

The following example illustrates focus on student content standards (e.g., Common Core) with differentiation embedded.

Standard: Content and Pedagogy

Quality professional learning enhances educators' expertise to increase students' capacity to learn and thrive.

Element A: Curriculum Content and Materials

Quality professional learning builds educators' knowledge and understanding of subject-matter curricula and materials so that all students meet content and performance expectations and are ready for college and careers.

Indicators: Quality professional learning:

1. Focuses on learning the content required in meeting state and district outcomes for students.

2. Deepens and extends subject-matter knowledge within educators' own discipline and across other disciplines.

3. Builds educators' capacity to use curriculum frameworks, instructional materials, equipment, and technology that support the teaching and learning of subject-matter content.

4. Increases educators' use of adaptive and linguistically and culturally responsive materials.

This example illustrates focus on differentiated responses, emphasizing traditionally underserved students: content standards (e.g., Common Core) with differentiation embedded:

Standard: Equity

Quality professional learning focuses on equitable access, opportunities, and outcomes for all students, with an emphasis on addressing achievement and opportunity disparities between student groups.

Element B: Systemic Equity

Quality professional learning helps educators develop equitable and inclusive policies and align them with implemented practices.

Indicators: Quality professional learning:

1. Ensures that all educators have equitable access to effective professional learning and support.

2. Highlights school and district policies that lead to systemic inequities for students, and addresses how to change those policies.

3. Identifies educational programs in which students are overrepresented or underrepresented in proportion to their percentage of a district or school's entire population, and helps educators deal with those inequities.

The national Standards for Professional Learning and the Superintendent's QPLS from California are two examples of guides for educator growth and development. Both illustrate how these standards highlight features that are most likely to lead to the results we want. When carefully constructed and used, they can work with student content standards, such as CCSS, to shine a light on purposefully coordinated student and educator learning that attends to students who have unique assets and needs.

CULTURALLY PROFICIENT PROFESSIONAL LEARNING

For the purpose of this book, we have taken the most prominent five themes from the national Standards for Professional Learning and the Superintendent's QPLS from California and created a graphic organizer presented as Table 6.2 in the next chapter to demonstrate the interdependent relationship of professional learning and the 5 Essential Elements of Cultural Proficiency. This graphic organizer shows the dynamic alignment of the actions of the Essential Elements with the standards for high-quality professional learning. Chapters 7–11 give descriptions of each of the Essential Elements paired with a standard to demonstrate the opportunities for implementation of Culturally Proficient Professional Learning.

What many of the new Common Core efforts are missing is direct attention to what will make the CCSS initiative more likely to get outcomes for all students. Attention to moving all students forward to graduate ready for success in college and careers—including those demographic groups usually underserved—requires using the lens of Culturally Proficiency along with effective leadership and continuous professional learning.

GOING DEEPER

Throughout this chapter we have reflected on how the Common Core presents us with opportunities as learners, educators, and leaders. Given what you now know, what are you rethinking about professional development/learning? What are your professional learning goals for this academic year? In what ways might you redesign your professional learning plan? What are you learning about yourself as an educator?

_____

_____

_____

_____

DIALOGIC ACTIVITY

To this point in the book, you and your colleagues have had the opportunity to review and, in some cases, to engage in new learning. In what ways does this chapter inform your continued professional learning? What new questions surface for your group as you anticipate professional learning over the next few years? What specific recommendations can you make to school leaders to inform them of your desires and needs?

_____

_____

_____

_____

Chapter 6 offers you the opportunity to use the lens of Cultural Proficiency and examine the standards of professional learning to ensure equity through the Common Core Standards. You now have the Tools of Cultural Proficiency, quality Professional Learning Standards, and the rationale for using Common Core Standards so that all students will be prepared for college and career choices. It's time to work through another opportunity in the next chapter by revisiting the notion of challenging mindsets and reframing for next steps.

6 From Stuckness to Implementation (or From Yikes! to YES!)

Change is possible when you acknowledge the obstacles but refuse to allow them to overwhelm you.

—John Baldoni, 2013

GETTING CENTERED

John Baldoni also acknowledged in his blog that change is easy as long as you are not the one being asked to change your beliefs or behaviors. So, think for minute about a time you were asked to change the way you behave, or change the way you assess student learning, or change the way you design lesson plans, or change the way you interact with parents and families of your students, or change the way you collaborate with other educators to design new curriculum to meet new standards. These are just a few of the changes the Common Core State Standards (CCSS) are asking many teachers and administrators to consider where appropriate. Now, think about your willingness to acknowledge the obstacles that keep you from being as effective as you want to be and your refusal to allow the obstacles to keep you from becoming the educator you need and want to be. What comes to mind for you as you think of change and changing? What will it take to move you and your colleagues forward? Please use the space below to record your thinking.

_____

_____

_____

_____

This chapter describes what happens when a school moves from being stuck to moving forward using the lens of Cultural Proficiency as an approach for changing behaviors and beliefs. As most of us know and have experienced, we cannot force another person to change. And, we have also learned from\past experience that rewards and sanctions do not produce the changes we want in schools (Fullan, 2011). However, the research on changing attitudes is clear—actions change first, followed by beliefs. Offering people new experiences can lead to new beliefs, which can lead to more purposeful actions. For example, the characters in this chapter take on new experiences as a result of professional learning experiences. As a result of those experiences, they are able to view their students in different ways with new beliefs forming as they interact with their students in new ways. The chapter also introduces a rubric (Table 6.1) that guides you in developing your Culturally Proficient Professional Learning Action Plan.

FROM YIKES! TO YES! ONE PRINCIPAL'S STORY

Cultural Proficiency embodies the personal values and behaviors of individuals and the organization's policies and practices that provide opportunities for effective multicultural interactions among students, educators, and community members. Culturally proficient educators value their school community and are shaped by its diversity. Using Cultural Proficiency as a mindset for their actions enables educators to respond to people effectively in cross-cultural environments by using a powerful set of interrelated tools to guide personal and organizational change (Lindsey, Nuri Robins, & Terrell, 2009). These Tools for culturally proficient practices allow site administrators and other school and district leaders to focus on assets to overcome barriers to student progress and success.

In Chapters 7 through 11, our middle school principal, Lupe, and other educators use the Four Tools of Cultural Proficiency to examine their own behaviors and their school's policies and practices. They intentionally plan their leadership actions for the implementation of quality professional learning that supports students being college and career ready upon high school graduation. First, Lupe took one tool, the Guiding Principles, and used each principle as a question to examine her own core values, beliefs, and assumptions about the diverse community she served; then, she examined the extent to which her leadership practices aligned with her espoused values. Lupe felt she needed to apply the Guiding Principles to her own work before she could ask her faculty to examine their belief systems and assumptions. She reflected on the following nine Guiding Principles for Cultural Proficiency:

1. *To what extent do you honor culture as a natural and normal part of the community you serve?*

2. *To what extent do you recognize and understand the differential and historical treatment accorded to those least well served in our schools?*

3. *When working with a person whose culture is different from yours, to what extent do you see the person as both an individual and as a member of a cultural group?*

4. *To what extent do you recognize and value the differences within the cultural communities you serve?*

5. *To what extent do you know and respect the unique needs of cultural groups in the community you serve?*

6. *To what extent do you know how cultural groups in your community define family and the manner in which family serves as the primary system of support for students?*

7. *To what extent do you recognize and understand the bicultural reality for cultural groups historically not well served in our schools?*

8. *To what extent do you recognize your role in acknowledging, adjusting to and accepting cross-cultural interactions as necessary social and communications dynamics?*

9. *To what extent do you incorporate cultural knowledge into educational practices and policy-making?*

(Lindsey, Terrell, Nuri, & Lindsey, 2010)

Lupe realized the Guiding Principles were cornerstones for confronting systemic and individual barriers to moving forward as a culturally proficient leader and school. She realized another Cultural Proficiency Tool, the Barriers to Cultural Proficiency, would be overcome only when these barriers were recognized as deeply held negative assumptions. These assumptions must be surfaced and confronted through intentional conversations and meaningful, well-focused, facilitated dialogue sessions. She moved forward by posing questions to prompt her own examination of the barrier questions:

- What might be some ways we are demonstrating resistance to implementing the Common Core?
- In what ways might **I** be more aware of our need to adapt to our changing community and student needs?
- In what ways might systemic oppression, or my understanding of it, be impacting or influencing **my** resistance toward moving forward?
- What might be some ways that the system and sense of privilege and entitlement are getting in **my** way of moving us forward?

Lupe had already begun confronting her own biases and barriers using these reflective questions. She realized that before the school could move forward in fully implementing the CCSS, the faculty would need to address issues of change and confront their own barriers and biases. She had recently heard faculty members talk about being "stuck in their ways" and afraid to move forward with the new standards. She had heard others talk about "Why change what we are doing? We do the best we can do with the kids that we have." And other comments ranged from, "What are we afraid of?" to "Why don't we take back our school and make the changes ourselves? We can do this!"

As she was preparing for the opening of the new school year, Lupe knew she needed to begin the academic year with a strong push forward. When she first thought about the implementation guidelines of the Common Core Standards that she received from the District Office, her response was, "Yikes!" Her faculty had been stuck in the No Child Left Behind (NCLB) standardized testing phase for the past 10 years. Their school scores had peaked, and the school had not experienced "test" growth for the past four years. African American, Latino, and low-income students groups were not achieving at similar levels as Asian and white students. Lupe had wanted to engage with the faculty in getting unstuck and move toward implementation of the CCSS in ways that would honor them as learners and teachers and at the same time confront the barriers that were keeping them from serving all students in their community. Lupe decided to use the lens of

Cultural Proficiency to frame the work of the CCSS. She decided to begin with the inside-out approach that she had used for her own work. Each faculty member received a summary article of *What Is Cultural Proficiency and How Will It Help Us Implement CCSS?* prior to the opening one-day Faculty Retreat. The article included the 9 Guiding Principles' Questions that Lupe had used for her own reflection weeks earlier. One of the first activities for the Faculty Retreat was called *Using the Guiding Principles to Confront our Barriers.* The faculty engaged in a facilitated dialogue using these questions as prompts:

- What might be some ways we are demonstrating resistance to implementing the Common Core?
- In what ways might **I/we** be more aware of our need to adapt to our changing community and student needs?
- In what ways might systemic oppression, or **my/our** understanding of it, be impacting or influencing **my/our** resistance toward moving forward?
- What might be some ways that the system and sense of privilege and entitlement are getting in **my/our** way of moving forward?

REFLECTION

What do you envision for dialogue sessions using these prompts? What might be additional questions to facilitate the dialogue for surfacing assumptions that are creating barriers and *stuckness* toward implementation of goals. In what ways might the Guiding Principles counterbalance these barriers?

_____

_____

_____

_____

WE'RE IN THIS TOGETHER: COLLECTIVE EFFICACY AND ACADEMIC OPTIMISM

Often in education we are called upon to implement new programs because of new legislation, new funding sources, or new personnel to our districts. The focus, then, centers on the program itself, rather than the people charged with implementing the program or those who might benefit from the program. The loyalty of the people who are charged with implementing the program focuses on the success or failure of the program, rather than on the learning needs of their colleagues. In contrast, when the focus is on people rather than programs, the result is a greater sense of trust and collaboration. People working together as a collective believe they can make a difference and trust they can reach their desired goals together. Hoy (2006) and his colleagues demonstrated that school faculty can come together in a collective, positive, academic environment when committed to three properties:

- School faculty believes it can teach even the most difficult students—collective efficacy
- School faculty trusts students and parents—faculty trust
- School faculty emphasizes academics—academic emphasis

They labeled this positive, academic environment *academic optimism*. Further research by McGuigan and Hoy (2006) and Smith and Hoy (2007) provided the connection between academic optimism and student achievement in urban and elementary schools.

Lupe and the school's teacher leaders working collaboratively in a trusting, positive, optimistic, academic environment would provide the foundation for implementing the Common Core State Standards as a transformative initiative in their school. As Linda Darling-Hammond (2012) stated, "The work of improving practice must therefore be conceptualized as collective rather than individual" (p. 36). To successfully transform traditionally "stuck" systems into schools that are prepared to move forward, leaders must develop new models structured to promote and support collaboration and knowledge building/sharing, rather than promote competition across the school and larger school district. Lupe realized that she must support her teacher leaders with professional learning that honors their strengths and supports their needs to meet the new standards. She found the following post in a leadership blog that informed her thinking:

> . . . *nurturing teacher leadership requires high trust and positive working relationships. Megan Tschannen-Moran described trust as the "invisible underpinning of collaboration and learning," underscoring the importance of human relationships in regard to positive school cultures. She noted that people have to work actively at gaining someone's trust. Establishing trusting and constructive relationships is a condition necessary in fostering teacher leadership.*

In The Moral Imperative of School Leadership, *Michael Fullan (2003) noted that leading schools required principals with the courage and capacity to build new cultures based on trusting relationships and a culture of disciplined inquiry and action. Fostering teacher leadership through collaborative inquiry just seems like the right place to start (DeWitt, 2013).*

With encouragement from most of her faculty following the opening of the school retreat, Lupe decided that it was time for educators to "take back our school," as one of her teachers had said. That phrase resonated with the faculty at the retreat, as teachers talked about making the CCSS "ours" rather than the traditional "top-down" change initiative. She carefully explained that the fiscal resources would be coming from federal, state, and district sources, so "we are all in this change initiative, together," she said. "And, we can take care of implementing the standards in ways that will best serve our school community," Lupe added.

She met with her Leadership Team, and, with considerable forethought, they intentionally and collaboratively established an Action Plan for Professional Learning in Support of Implementing CCSS. She told the team, "Let's move from 'Yikes!' to 'Yes!' and move forward with our plan." Lupe knew the way to address the needs of the teachers and their students was to support the teachers through high-quality, standards-based, Culturally Proficient Professional Learning.

CULTURALLY PROFICIENT PROFESSIONAL LEARNING: OUTCOMES = EDUCATOR PERFORMANCE

To meet and exceed learner achievement standards by 2014 as required by No Child Left Behind (NCLB, 2002), educators and policymakers realized student performance expectations must be aligned with curriculum that is aligned with content standards. Instructors identify and use instructional strategies aligned with those content and performance standards, select materials of instruction that supported all learners, and use assessment data to inform their teaching practices so that more learners will achieve at levels higher than ever before. Achievement by all learners was the underlying assumption for standards-based education from 2001–2014. However, prior to reaching the target dates of 2014, educators and policymakers realized the academic targets were not being reached by many school districts, and the achievement gap was not closing between students of color and their white and Asian counterparts (Zacarian, 2013).

For all learners to be successful, educators must know and understand how learners learn and develop, how learners differ in their approaches to learning, and how to develop learning opportunities that are adapted to diverse learners. The culturally proficient instructor uses learners' diverse experiences, perspectives, and learning styles to create a teaching and learning environment that is respectful of each learner and encourages positive social interaction and active engagement in learning and self-motivation. In today's richly diverse classrooms, educators must develop new approaches and acquire new skills while at the same time learn to connect with the students in their classrooms in new and different ways (Pappano, 2010; Wilmore, 2002). For some educators, these behaviors required a shift in thinking from the traditional "subject-based curriculum" approach to a learner-centered, standards-based approach (Armstrong, Henson, & Savage, 2005; Voltz, Sims, & Nelson, 2010). Although the national attention has been on standards-based instruction for well over a decade, all instructors and educational leaders have not embraced a standards-based instructional model.

NCLB's remedy for inequity required scientifically proven instruction strategies and new standards for student performance and accountability. The shift in thinking and teaching, however, seemed to be from standards-based instruction to standardized test results. Although the intent of President George W. Bush's No Child Left Behind Act of 2001 was to address the persistent problems of inequity, racism, and prejudice in PK–12 schools, the mandate did not meet the goals. Perhaps we learned something from NCLB about change initiatives and reform, namely that government mandates and required timelines do not result in totally closing the academic gaps that have been well documented for more than 40 years in the United States (National Assessment of Educational Progress, 2007). However, portions of NCLB did call attention to the need for changes in the system that traditionally served some students better than others. The national initiative, however, could not mandate the moral imperative to serve all learners in ways to narrow and close those gaps. We need to go deeper to ask *why?* Why should we as educators focus on the way we teach as well as what we teach?

CHANGE AS AN INSIDE-OUT PROCESS BEGINS WITH "WHY?"

Today's complex classrooms and the introduction of the CCSS require instructors to not only think about their *mental model* for teaching, but also to consider alternative ways of determining learner outcomes, preparing lessons, selecting materials, presenting lessons, and assessing learner performance. The CCSS requires educators to align the new educational policies (i.e., every student will be college and career ready by 12th grade) with the curriculum, instructional practices, and the assessment tools and strategies they are using. Linked to each of these alignments is an examination of educators' and schools' assumptions about and need for inclusion, collaboration, resources, leadership, and professional learning.

To successfully implement the CCSS school district policymakers, administrators, teachers, and community members must recognize one of the barriers they will confront is the general resistance to change. The Change Leadership Group under the guidance of Tony Wagner from Harvard's School of Education spent years 2001 through 2008 studying selected school districts that were implementing change initiatives from the No Child Left Behind Act of 2001. These scholars distinguish between technical challenges versus adaptive challenges that must be confronted to bring about necessary results. Wagner and his co-writers relied on Ron Heifetz's descriptions of technical and adaptive challenges:

> *A technical challenge is one for which a solution is already known—the knowledge and capacity exist to solve the problem. . . .*
>
> *An 'adaptive' challenge, on the other hand, is one for which the necessary knowledge to solve the problem does not yet exist. It requires creating the knowledge and the tools to solve the problem* in the act of working on it.
>
> (Wagner et al., 2006, p. 10)

Therefore, both the organization and the leader(s) experiences changes in who they are and who they become during the process of *working on it*. Wagner et al. (2006) emphasize that this kind of change is actually transformative in nature and requires leaders to confront these adaptive challenges by becoming "knowledge-generating" versus "knowledge-using" organizations. Leaders of these transformative schools and districts must first do their own work of examining their own values, beliefs, behaviors, and assumptions about who gets left behind and who moves ahead before they can expect the whole organization to change how they deliver services to the students and their communities (Lindsey, Roberts, & CampbellJones, 2013; Wagner, et al., 2006).

Cross (1989) describes Cultural Proficiency as an *inside-out* process of both individual and organizational change. The change process Cross describes is intentional. We become mindful of our individual beliefs, values, and assumptions that lead to our behaviors. As members of organizations serving diverse communities, we are willing to intentionally engage with others to closely question and examine our espoused values, beliefs, and assumptions about the cultural and demographic groups we serve to see if they match our plans and actions. The questions that guide this inside-out approach are:

Who am I as an educator?

Am I who I say I am?

Who are we as an organization?

Are we who we say we are?

Examining our intentions and confronting a shift for our thinking as we prepare for transformative professional learning is to ask the *Why* question. Wagner et al. (2006) presented this compelling view of inside-out thinking that dovetails well with Cross's (1989) inside-out approach to personal and institutional change:

We believe the successful leadership of transformational improvement processes in schools and districts requires sharpening capacities in two quite different directions at the same time:

- *Leaders need to see more deeply into why it is so hard for our organizations to change, even when there is a genuine, collective desire to do so. More than just seeing why, leaders need to learn how to take action effectively to help our organizations actually become what they need and want to be.*
- *Leaders need to see more deeply into why it is so hard for individuals to change, even when individuals intend to do so. Beyond this merely diagnostic self-understanding, we as leaders need to learn how to take action effectively to help ourselves become the person we need and want to be in order to better serve the children and families of our communities. (p. xvi)*

REFLECTION

Take a few minutes and describe the inside-out approach in your own words. How might you describe *who* you are? Are you who you say you are? What might be data/artifacts that you would use to demonstrate who you are aligned with your beliefs and values?

PROFESSIONAL LEARNING AS A CHANGE FORCE

Teams of teachers working together can establish appropriate criteria, select complex tasks, and develop multiple approaches that provide diverse students opportunities for authentic responses to multiple assessments and standards-based performance tasks. These authentic student responses are often grounded in culture-based experiences. Professional learning that is designed to address educators' beliefs and values about their students' culture-based experiences can be the change force that leads the entire school toward closing academic and performance gaps on standards-based assessments.

Effective teachers realize that culture influences their own actions as well as the thoughts and behaviors of their students. To ignore the impact of one's culture is to ignore opportunities and challenges within the instructional teaching and learning environment. As noted by Voltz and colleagues (2010), the rich cultural diversity of classrooms provides teachers opportunities such as they and their:

- Students learn languages, customs, and worldviews from other students.
- Students develop cross-cultural competence and open-mindedness to new and different ways of seeing, knowing, and doing.
- Students prepare for the global reality of their future work world.

The learner is the center of the teacher's world. A culturally proficient instructor knows and values the importance of standards-based instruction. The overarching goal of enhancing educational outcomes for all learners means *all* learners. Embracing student diversity, including all abilities and languages, requires teachers to hold high expectations for each and every student. High expectations are implicit in standards-based instruction and hold particular importance in culturally proficient educational practices (Voltz, Sims, & Nelson, 2010).

A school and district's commitment to standards for professional learning is an important first step. A set of professional standards suggest equity, in that educators across a school or district agree to follow a common framework, or guidelines, that manifests itself through equitable opportunities for all learners. When professional learning standards are in place, a commitment by educators means a commitment to best practices and expertise in support of all educators improving their practice in ways to better serve all learners (Hord & Roy, 2014).

Professional learning standards also provide common language across schools, districts, states, and the nation. Educators can engage in planning conversations, share materials, monitor results, and change their practice using a common set of professional learning standards for growth and account-ability for themselves and their students (Hord & Roy, 2014). Integrate the framework of Cultural Proficiency with the professional learning stand-ards, and educators have the best of both worlds for addressing equity and access of all students to be college and career ready when they graduate from high school.

To reach these long-term goals for student outcomes, instructors must search for resources, support, and opportunities to include subject area and content standards that focus on the diverse needs of learners; textbooks that include global perspectives and multicultural experiences; and instructor-led strategies that build communities within the classrooms. Professional learning programs that include multicultural instructional strategies, selec-tion of appropriate materials, and multiple assessment strategies support the instructors' efforts to grow and meet the needs of diverse learners in today's complex classrooms.

In an editorial published in the *Los Angeles Times* (2014), the writer offered the following changes for the CCSS to be more effective:

- Recognize that Common Core, though it has many features in its favor, isn't necessarily perfect. There needs to be more willingness at the federal and state levels to listen to legitimate concerns and to allow for flexibility when the standards' ideals don't match up with reality.
- States and schools should be given a few years to implement the standards. Teacher training and textbooks need to be in place.
- Schools and teachers should not be held accountable for standard-ized test scores for the first few years; rather, test scores should be used solely to guide future instruction as everyone adjusts. There will almost certainly be kinks to work out.

RESOURCES TO SUPPORT PROFESSIONAL LEARNING

As schools and districts move toward implementation planning for ini-tiatives such as the Common Core, consideration must be given to cost factors and equitable availability of resources. Nowhere is the question of equity more obvious than that of technology to support the assessments that measure student performance against the Common Core Standards. Since assessments drive decisions about curriculum materials and instruc-tion strategies, these performance assessments will have a strong influence on whether or how schools make the necessary changes for students to achieve at standards level (Rothman, 2013).

Assessments aligned with the Common Core, such as the Partnership for Assessment of Readiness for College and Careers—a group of states and the District of Columbia—and the Smarter Balanced Assessment Consortium, represent a significant departure from the NCLB standardized "bubble test." The performance assessments ask students to apply their knowledge of math and English language arts rather than recall information and choose possible responses. The new assessments require students to use higher order thinking skills and complex analyses (Rothman, 2013). For students to perform well on these assessments, educators must be well prepared to instruct students using methods and materials that support their students complex, higher order learning. The assessment consortia worked with their member states to develop online assessment tasks aligned with classroom instruction (Rothman, 2013). Questions that must be considered as equity issues related to assessments are: Will the technology be in place for all students to access the online assessment strategies prior to the final assessments? In what ways will districts share resources to ensure equitable access for all learners and educators?

The biggest tasks, of course, are for member states to develop and share materials of instruction that are aligned with the CCSS. Unfortunately, early indicators are that the field hasn't produced enough good instructional materials aligned with the CCSS; therefore, educators are struggling to create their own. Studies are also showing that professional learning is too quick and too shallow, and educators are finding students are approaching time to take tests that are not aligned to what they are being taught (Gewertz, 2014). Although many textbook companies advertise their books to be "Common Core aligned," a researcher recently called them "snake oil salesmen" and said that 60 percent to 70 percent of the textbooks are identical to pre–Common Core texts. However, publishers protest those findings and encourage districts to be good consumers of Common Core materials. Some of the textbook companies hire experts who worked on developing the Common Core standards as their textbook consultants to ensure alignment (Herold & Molnar, 2014). In what ways are materials of instruction being developed in your district and schools? Will all students have access to materials aligned with the CCSS and the new performance assessments?

TWIN GOALS: ACHIEVING QUALITY PROFESSIONAL LEARNING THROUGH THE LENS OF CULTURAL PROFICIENCY

If the Common Core promise of better outcomes for all students is to be fulfilled, all educators must commit not only to academic excellence but also to equity. This means that educators need to build a cache of instructionally focused strategies that enables them to address new student standards requiring deeper, specialized knowledge of pedagogy based in research, new technologies, better formative assessments, and improved ways of serving our diverse student population. It also means that educators are required to learn how to productively collaborate with colleagues and experts; develop expertise in designing and modifying curricula and instruction based on evidence of student progress; monitor and adjust implementation and change processes; and provide constructive, differentiated feedback for ongoing improvement. Furthermore, to ensure this iteration of standards-based instruction yields results that reduce and eliminate student achievement disparities, professional learning requires leaders to fuse approaches to improve student academic achievement with the Essential Elements of Cultural Proficiency. Professional learning standards are the bedrock of quality professional learning and together with the Essential Elements form the foundation for Culturally Proficient Professional Learning.

The Tools for Cultural Proficiency (Chapter 3) are designed to guide individuals and organizations to examine their values and behaviors based on their beliefs and assumptions about how students learn and who can learn. This is the inside-out approach for changing behaviors and environments. Once an organization's members examine who they are and for whose purpose they exist, they have a greater chance of developing skills and capabilities to address the behaviors and environments within the organization. When a professional learning program is consistent with the organization's identity/vision and beliefs, educators share the responsibility of developing resources in support of those agreed upon components of the Professional Learning Plan.

One way to develop a Culturally Proficient Learning Plan is to use Table 6.1, A Rubric for Cultural Proficiency Professional Learning in Support of the Common Core Standards, to examine the school's or district's healthy/unhealthy and productive/unproductive values, language, and behaviors placed along the Continuum. The three cells on the left (negative side of the Continuum) are informed by the Barriers, and the three cells on the right (positive side of the Continuum) are informed by the Guiding Principles. Remember from the discussion of the Tools in Chapter 3, the standards of action are met at the Cultural Competence level on the rubric.

Table 6.1 indicates actions and behaviors based on deeply held assumptions and values about professional learning. The three cells on the right are aligned with professional learning for educators seeking to support all students having access to a common core of knowledge, instruction activities, materials, and assessment strategies.

Table 6.1 Rubric for Cultural Proficiency Professional Learning in Support of the Common Core Standards

Outcome: Increase the achievement and well-being of all students, with an emphasis on addressing achievement and opportunity disparities between student groups, by continuously improving the knowledge, skills, and attitudes of educators who educate and support them.

5 Essential Elements serve as standards for Culturally Proficient Leadership	Informed by Barriers to Cultural Proficiency Tolerance for Diversity: *Focus on "Them"*			Informed by the Guiding Principles of Cultural Proficiency Transformation for Equity: *Focus on "Our Practice"*		
	Cultural Destructiveness	**Cultural Incapacity**	**Cultural Blindness**	**Cultural Precompetence**	**Cultural Competence**	**Cultural Proficiency**
Assessing Cultural Knowledge identifies the differences among people in your environment; be aware of the importance of cultural identity; identify organizational culture.	**Professional learning** reinforces cultural misinformation that "we are all the same" by training educators in a single/ one-size-fits-all approach to instruction and student learning.	**Professional learning** uses information about student differences as the rationale for training teachers to "get all students on board" in reaching a target considered the norm.	**Professional learning** focuses on generalized best practices for standards-based instruction that apply to all educators and students, without differentiation.	**Culturally Proficient Professional Learning** begins to reference disaggregated student and educator data about culture and CCSS capacity in order to identify strengths and improvement areas and determine individual and collective learning priorities.	**And . . .** actively engages educators in learning about their own cultures and examining their personal attitudes and biases in relation to staff, student, and school cultures to determine how their own assets and needs may support or hinder student success in being college and career ready.	**And . . .** integrates opportunities in real tasks to practice increased cultural knowledge about using relevant, disaggregated student and educator data to inform differentiated, culturally relevant instruction that supports students in being college and career ready.

(Continued)

Table 6.1 (Continued)

	Informed by Barriers to Cultural Proficiency Tolerance for Diversity: *Focus on "Them"*			Informed by the Guiding Principles of Cultural Proficiency Transformation for Equity: *Focus on "Our Practice"*		
Valuing Diversity embraces differences as contributors to the value of your environment; address cultural experiences and opportunities.	**Professional learning** is based on developing educators' skills in removing or punishing diverse student culture, language, etc., in order to help students become successful.	**Professional learning** focuses on developing educators' skills to standardize student language, learning approaches, etc., to meet expectations of the dominant culture.	**Professional learning** reinforces strategies that lead educators "not to play favorites," resulting in their ignoring cultural and linguistic diversity and providing all educators and/or students with the same instruction and support.	**Culturally Proficient Professional Learning** recognizes that educator diversity can extend professional knowledge and understanding of staff and student cultures and experiences that can help students make connections to learning and a variety of pathways to academic success.	**And . . .** encourages educators to work collaboratively to learn new instructional and cultural competency skills to increase the variety of approaches effective for students with a range of assets and needs to learn and thrive.	**And . . .** relies on educators' diverse cultures, experiences, and capabilities to develop and lead staff learning and the application of differentiated instructional and support strategies required for each student to meet expectations of the Common Core.

	Informed by Barriers to Cultural Proficiency Tolerance for Diversity: *Focus on "Them"*		Informed by the Guiding Principles of Cultural Proficiency Transformation for Equity: *Focus on "Our Practice"*		
Managing the Dynamics of Difference	**Professional learning**	**Professional learning**	**Culturally Proficient Professional Learning**	**And . . .**	**And . . .**
reframes differences so diversity is not perceived as a problem to be solved; promotes models using inquiry, dialogue related to multiple perspectives, and issues arising from diversity.	does not acknowledge diversity issues but helps educators' learn how to solve people problems and quickly activate a uniform response "to keep the lid" on a challenging situation.	poses diversity as a challenge that can be addressed with a foolproof solution that is "tried and true."	identifies and/or structures opportunities for educators to learn, practice inquiry, and dialogue models that help them confidently address issues arising from multiple perspectives.	leads to the development of communities of practice where educators use inquiry and dialogue models to reframe anticipated or current issues they are facing in implementing equitable practices to address CCSS expectations.	enables educators to find ways to provide students with a range of instructional approaches and supports that fit their diverse set of assets and needs and meet different student, family, and institutional expectations so that every student graduates college and career ready.
		poses problems of practice that minimize the importance of multiple perspectives and highlight reaching consensus for the common good in order to avoid discussions about diversity that may be uncomfortable.			

(Continued)

Table 6.1 (Continued)

	Informed by Barriers to Cultural Proficiency Tolerance for Diversity: *Focus on "Them"*			Informed by the Guiding Principles of Cultural Proficiency Transformation for Equity: *Focus on "Our Practice"*		
Adapting to Diversity	**Professional learning**	**Professional learning**	**Professional learning**	**Culturally Proficient Professional Learning**	**And . . .**	**And . . .**
teaches and learns about differences and how to respond to them effectively; facilitates change to meet the needs of the community.	is not differentiated or purposefully connected to educator, student, or community needs.	emphasizes how educators can maintain the status quo to sustain "stability" that students can count on.	is organized as a common opportunity for all educators and consists mainly of approved programs provided by regional, state, or federal providers.	helps educators develop understanding about instructional changes required by the new Common Core Standards, determine current capacities and needs to implement equity-focused policies and practices, and initiate ongoing educator learning and support to develop expertise and confidence.	extends educator experiences related to a variety of equity perspectives, including race, gender, language, sexual orientation, religion, special abilities and needs, and socioeconomic status that may impact students' initial ability to meet CCSS expectations.	promotes collective action to develop and apply policies and practices that support the wide variety of instruction and support services required by diverse students engaged in meeting CCSS standards and moving toward college and careers.

	Informed by Barriers to Cultural Proficiency			Informed by the Guiding Principles of Cultural Proficiency		
	Tolerance for Diversity: *Focus on "Them"*			Transformation for Equity: *Focus on "Our Practice"*		
Institutionalizing Cultural Knowledge	**Professional learning**	**Professional learning**	**Professional learning**	**Culturally Proficient Professional Learning**	**And . . .**	**And . . .**
changes systems to ensure healthy and effective responses to diversity; shape policies and practices that meet the needs of a diverse community.	does not reflect student or educator diversity or address how differentiated support is necessary to implement practices that lead to CCSS implementation.	supports approaches that reinforce values and policies ensuring that assimilation is applied in classrooms and schools.	opportunities are mandated, reflecting the belief that common approaches can serve the needs of all cultural groups.	provides the means for educators to learn about and practice theories and principles of equity that can support or hinder culturally responsive policies and actions related to student learning success.	promotes educators' developing the structure and processes for an ongoing, comprehensive system of individual and collective learning that responds to diverse and changing educator and student needs with reliable supports to meet CCSS expectations that every student graduates ready to be successful in college or a career.	includes educators' reviewing individual and collective professional learning experiences and results over time to evaluate whether professional learning efforts and changes in policies and practices are having an impact on educator effectiveness and, ultimately, all students' performance and well-being.

Table 6.2 demonstrates our integrated approach to align and integrate the 5 Essential Elements of Cultural Proficiency (on the left margin of Table 6.1) with Standards for Quality Professional Learning (SQPLs). These SQPLs were developed as composite themes from the Learning Forward Professional Learning Standards and the California Quality Professional Learning Standards (California Department of Education, 2013).

Table 6.2 Integrated Approach for Culturally Proficient Professional Learning Standards

Essential Elements for Culturally Proficient Practices in Support of Common Core	Standards for Quality Professional Learning in Support of Common Core
Assessing cultural knowledge	Collecting, analyzing, and using data to guide decisions
Valuing diversity	Developing skillful leaders to create support systems for professional learning
Managing the dynamics of difference	Creating and sustaining learning communities
Adapting to diversity	Applying evidence-based approaches to actively engage educators in improving practice
Institutionalizing cultural knowledge	Applying and connecting a common commitment toward common outcomes for all students

The 5 Essential Elements and the SQPLs in Table 6.2 are the frames for the development of a Common Core Professional Learning Action Plan in Chapters 7–11. One of the characters in the Middletown story, the principal, Lupe, continues to lead her faculty from Yikes! to YES! by examining their professional learning activities through the lens of Cultural Proficiency using the rubric in Table 6.1 and the frames from Table 6.2. The Middletown stories are told in the following chapters.

GOING DEEPER

Using the 5 Essential Elements, what might be some actions you would include in your daily instructional life to ensure alignment with your espoused values and beliefs about how students learn and how you teach? As you examine Table 6.1, what actions can the principal take to lead teachers and staff across the continuum? Choose one of the Essential Elements you'd like to think more about. Read the descriptions across the element, from Cultural Destructiveness to Cultural Proficiency (from left to right). Where are you/your school?

_____

_____

_____

_____

DIALOGIC ACTIVITY

With a group of your colleagues, engage in a dialogue to continue your shared understanding of *a school culture in support of all learners performing at levels higher than ever before*. In what ways does the rubric inform your understanding of equity and implementation of the Common Core? What is currently in place in your school that supports implementation? What are two or three things yet to be done? Continue the dialogue throughout small learning communities in the school district. Once shared understanding has been reached, what might be some resources, strategies, and structures that could be developed and activated to support all learners, with emphasis on *college and career readiness*? How might members of your department or school respond to the questions *Who are we?* and *Are we who we say we are?* What might be some artifacts you would display to demonstrate the alignment of your actions with your espoused values and beliefs?

CULTURALLY PROFICIENT PROFESSIONAL LEARNING, CHAPTERS 7–11

The following five chapters present authentic examples of educators using the integration of Cultural Proficiency's 5 Essential Elements with 5 Standards for Quality Professional Learning. Each chapter pairs an essential element with a professional learning standard as an illustration of the power and purpose of acting in an intentional way to implement the Common Core State Standards as a systems approach for change. The illustrations are composite case stories from situations in which the authors worked and/or were aware of educators' engagement in implementation of culturally proficient educational practices.

Part II

Culturally Proficient Professional Learning

Y ou are invited and challenged in the five chapters that comprise Part II to learn and apply the Essential Elements of Cultural Proficiency. Chapters 7 through 11 each describe one Essential Element by defining and discussing the Essential Element as a standard for professional practice that informs and clarifies educator values and behaviors as well as school policy development and practice. This is not a linear, one-for-one use of an Essential Element, but rather a holistic approach of the Essential Elements as found in the rubric in Chapter 6. We present the Essential Elements in separate chapters to facilitate deep study and mastery of each element as a standard for professional practice. Each Element is paired with a theme for Quality Professional Learning Standards. We pair an element with a standard for the purpose of illustrating the dynamics of using Cultural Proficiency as a lens to examine professional learning strategies to improve teaching and learning.

Chapter 12 is yours! You have the opportunity and the invitation to design your Culturally Proficient Professional Learning Action Plan. The Essential Elements are presented in a cohesive manner for individual educators and groups of educators to address ways to successfully educate all students in an equitable fashion that seeks to close access and achievement gaps. Chapter 12 guides you to be reflective, action oriented, and proactive in using the new language of Cultural Proficiency yourself and with your colleagues.

Assessing Cultural Knowledge

Collecting, Analyzing, and Using Data to Guide Decisions

Focus on equity begins with understanding students as individuals. This information is important to everyone working with students. What are their backgrounds? What are their perceptions and interests? What supports do they have at home?

—Gleason & Gerzon, 2013, p. 123

GETTING CENTERED

As you read the quote above, what information do you have about your students? What do you know about their backgrounds, interests, and perceptions? Now, think about your colleagues. What do you know about their backgrounds, expertise, interests, and perceptions? Take a few minutes and think about the benefits of knowing your students and your colleagues.

_____

_____

_____

_____

ASSESSING CULTURAL KNOWLEDGE
THROUGH COLLECTING AND ANALYZING DATA

The purpose of this chapter is to present quality professional learning viewed through the lens of Cultural Proficiency. Culturally Proficient Professional Learning (CPPL) examines various sources of data to inform decisions about teaching, learning, assessment, selection of materials, and shaping curriculum and instruction strategies. For example, when you and your colleagues collect and analyze disaggregated data of students' academic performances, you are able to focus on the importance of your practice and areas for professional growth that will impact all learners. Under the mandates of the No Child Left Behind (NCLB) Act of 2002, often the goal of some professional plans was to focus on improving the scores of the "bubble students," those closest to moving up to the next standardized scoring level. That method, however, did not impact the quality of educator effectiveness throughout the school, nor did it improve overall student performance.

CPPL AND STUDENT NEEDS

The intent of the CPPL approach is to use multiple measures, including formative and summative student achievement data, disaggregated by race, gender, language, special needs, and socioeconomic indicators for the purposes of identifying support systems for your students. The lens of Cultural Proficiency also includes mining family and community data in ways that include focus groups, family surveys, home visits, and community events. The information doesn't stop there. Possibly the school community members who know your students the best are staff members who work in the office, supervise students at lunch and in the parking and play areas, drive the busses, and prepare meals for students. The data from these multiple sources inform you and fellow educators about your students, their strengths and capabilities, the assets they bring to school, and their academic and social needs. Using the lens of Cultural Proficiency engages you in assessing your own cultural knowledge as well as the knowledge of the culture and climate of your school.

CPPL AND EDUCATOR NEEDS

You and your colleagues also depend on multiple sources of data to determine your professional strengths, assets, expertise, and needs. An effective professional learning plan includes survey data, focus group data, feedback loops, self-assessment data, and gap analyses between content knowledge and pedagogy. A Cultural Proficiency lens adds opportunities for you to assess your cultural knowledge about who you are as an educator. What are your attitudes toward professional growth? What do you believe might be reasons some students are not achieving at performance standards? You may also join your colleagues and assess your cultural knowledge as a school. What are our attitudes about professional learning? What do we believe might be some reasons some students are not performing at grade level? What do we do with the information and data that we have?

MOVE TO ACTION

Table 7.1 later in this chapter displays the actions consistent with the Essential Element of Assessing Cultural Knowledge integrated with data collection and analyses. As you think of your practice and your school's context, culturally proficient professional learning activities may include, but are not limited to:

- Design an *Inquiry* or *Action Research Project* that focuses on collecting data about our community and our students related to performance data.
- Lead a session on the decision-making process at the school.
- Collect and display artifacts (signage, icons, sports symbols, yearbooks, photos, etc.) that reflect student groups, community diversity, global perspectives, sense of welcome, and so on.
- Faculty and staff share *Cultural Autobiographies* as part of professional learning experiences.
- Assess the community assets through conversations with community elders and partners.
- Conduct focus groups and community surveys data collection and analyses to help determine community assets and expectations.
- Present results of community engagement conversations and feedback.

These are only a few actions that culturally proficient leaders can take to help determine the needs of the school community. Once the needs are determined, the professional learning goals and expectations can be determined. Professional learning that is focused on meeting needs of students so they will all be college and career ready is the hope and promise of the Common Core State Standards.

Lupe's story, begun in Chapter 6, is an example of the importance of collecting multiple sources of data and establishing a safe environment for conversations about the data. Table 7.1 is derived from the rubric presented in Chapter 6, Table 6.1. Each of the Chapters 7–11 will continue to take us back to Table 6.1 and illustrate the appropriate essential element.

Take a moment and read the definition in the first cell—Essential Element, Assessing Cultural Knowledge. Now read the next three cells to the right. Notice the sequence from precompetence, to competence, to proficiency. Take specific note of the mindful development on part of the leaders at the school—practicing, using, and applying. Take a few minutes and study Table 7.1.

What is your response to the illustrations in Table 7.1? In what ways does this confirm your understanding of professional learning communities? In what ways does the information in the table inform your understanding of this essential element, *Assessing Cultural Knowledge*? How might this information be useful to you at your school? Please use the space below to record your thoughts and questions.

_____

_____

_____

_____

ACTIONS INFORMED BY THE GUIDING PRINCIPLES OF CULTURAL PROFICIENCY

We demonstrate the importance of assessing cultural knowledge through collecting and analyzing data as part of a school leader's actions grounded in the Guiding Principles of Cultural Proficiency. Our middle school principal, Lupe Estrada, is preparing professional learning activities for the beginning-of-the-year faculty retreat. She and the faculty and staff ended the school year knowing the Common Core Standards were ready for implementation throughout the district. Some of her fellow principals were worried that things were moving too quickly, while others were

Table 7.1	Assessing Cultural Knowledge Through Data Collection and Analyses		
Informed by Guiding Principles of Cultural Proficiency **Transformation for Equity:** *Focus on "Our Practice"*			
Assessing Cultural Knowledge identifies the differences among people in your environment; be aware of the importance of cultural identity; identify organizational culture.	**Culturally Proficient Professional Learning** begins to reference disaggregated student and educator data about culture and CCSS capacity in order to identify strengths and improvement areas and determine individual and collective learning priorities.	**And . . .** actively engages educators in learning about their own cultures and examining their personal attitudes and biases in relation to staff, student and school cultures to determine how their own assets and needs may support or hinder student success in being college and career ready.	**And . . .** integrates opportunities in real tasks to practice increased cultural knowledge about using relevant, disaggregated student and educator data to inform differentiated, culturally relevant instruction that supports students in being college and career ready.

concerned that not enough was being done to provide the professional development to fully implement the new standards. Lupe had spent her summer weeks talking with her leadership team to get a sense of how they felt about the implementation time line for professional development. She recalled her "Yikes! to Yes!" plan as she thought about the opening of school year. Let's listen as she talks with her leadership team member, Sarah.

Lupe   *Well, Sarah, the first professional development session of the school year has arrived. As always, the agenda appears to be clear: Review the data from the last spring's testing. For Central View Middle, the news is not exhilarating, but not altogether depressing either. We jumped up a few points and a few points down depending on the subject you review. The overall trend, however, is abundantly clear. In the past four years, CVMS has been a flat line. Our API has hardly moved.*

Sarah   *Yeah, but Lupe, remember, interestingly, five years ago, we made a significant leap of 32 points. That was a huge growth for us!*

Lupe   *Yes, but then we got stuck. I'm going to meet with the department chairs and review ways to explore the data at the upcoming professional development session. Rather than presenting an interpretation of the data, I'm going to ask each department to analyze the data. What do you think about these essential questions for the foundation of the discussion?*

- Who are our students?
- What do we really know about the students who are not performing at and above grade level?
- What are the strengths and assets our students bring? For subject areas? From each demographic group?
- What are areas of concerns that need to be addressed from each demographic group?
- What are the implications for areas to be addressed this year in our instruction so that we are preparing for CCSS?
- What professional development do we want to better address the needs of all our students through the CCSS?

Sarah   *Well, these are certainly interesting questions. We'll get some interesting conversations from the Leadership Team, I'm sure. Then what?*

Lupe   *Well, as a Leadership Team, we lead! We will design the first day for meaningful conversations about professional development and our work with Cultural Proficiency. The Leadership Team is ready to present what they have learned about the Tools of Cultural Proficiency. We start the book study next week. What better time than now to begin this work? We are ready to move forward with CCSS through the lens of Cultural Proficiency.*

The questions that Lupe posed appear broad and somewhat general. However, they provide an open and safe environment to begin the conversation about the school's students and their needs. The Leadership Team continued to plan the Faculty Retreat full-day session to include activities for faculty members to get to know each other in ways they had not before. *What's in a Name, Cultural Perceptions, My Story*, and other learning activities demonstrated support for adult learners as well as provided strategies the teachers could use in their classrooms (Lindsey, Nuri Robins, & Terrell, 2009).

As the Leadership Team revealed the student data and facilitated the analyses process with the large group, Lupe encouraged the teachers to discuss how they viewed the data and how they felt about the students in the demographic groups. These emotional discussions revealed some feelings about the challenges implied in the data.

Sal	*You know, in the end, all this data is meaningless. It is telling us the same thing over and over. Some kids can and some kids can't. I am tired of being called on the carpet about this. I work hard, and the bottom line is kids who care, care, and those who don't, don't.*
Angela	*I used to feel that way, Sal. If some kids don't care about education, how can I make them care about the test? Yes, the test scores go up a little, we go down a little, but it is all the same. After today, maybe I'm the one who needs to think a bit differently. What do I really know about my kids? Not much! And, I really don't know much about their families. I just assumed their parents didn't care. I never really asked. I think I need to ask myself some more questions.*
Erik	*Well, I see the African American students dropped quite a bit, by five points. But, I don't really know why. I just accepted that as "the way they are." Sounds pretty lame now that I say that out loud. I need to know more.*
Alicia	*Maybe this is the best we can do. Well, you know, for the kids we have here at CVMS. Aren't we all doing the best we can do? There is nothing else that we can do, huh?*
Lupe	*Well, yes, there is. We are not giving up on our kids and we are not giving up on ourselves. We are going to use the new initiative of the Common Core Standards and the Tools of Cultural Proficiency to educate ourselves and grow professionally. We've been doing a good job, but now we have an opportunity to do even better. We are taking back this school from being compliant and we will move forward to excellence! We need to commit to this moving forward together. The CCSS are a set of guidelines for us to design our own plans so that our students can be on their way to high school graduation ready for college and career. Now, let's figure out how we can do this together!*

After the retreat, several teachers came by Lupe's office and commented on how "interesting and motivating" the day's session had been. She asked if they were interested enough to commit to moving forward with the planning. The responses were overwhelmingly positive. Over the next several days and weeks, Lupe would discover her own level of commitment to her journey toward Cultural Proficiency.

REFLECTION

As you reflect on the case story, what are your impressions of the conversation Lupe had with Sarah? In what ways are Lupe's behaviors consistent with the Essential Element of Assessing Cultural Knowledge? What might be additional data the faculty could collect about their students? What might be additional data the faculty could collect about themselves? Take a few minutes and write your thoughts and reactions and questions in the spaces below.

_____

_____

_____

_____

GOING DEEPER

Consider the dynamic of *assessing* and what it means in today's context of schooling. Does that word hold a positive or negative connotation for you? For your colleagues? In what ways does *assessing cultural knowledge* cause you to think differently about your students? About their communities? In these times of data-rich or data-overloaded environments, what might be additional data that you could collect that would better inform you and your colleagues about your students and their families?

DIALOGIC ACTIVITY

With a group of your colleagues, engage in a dialogue to reach shared understanding of a school culture *in support of assessing cultural knowledge through collecting and analyzing data.* Continue the dialogue throughout small learning communities in your school and district. Once shared understanding has been reached, what might be some resources, strategies, and structures that could be developed and activated to support all learners, with emphasis on *college and career readiness*? What might be some ways to assess cultural knowledge of your school and the community it serves? In what ways might that knowledge support professional learning for your school? Take a few minutes to write your responses in the spaces provided below.

_____

_____

_____

_____

Chapter 8 presents a case story illustrating the importance of valuing diversity by developing support systems through the school's professional learning plan. An elementary school principal works with teachers to design curriculum that is aligned with Common Core standards. The chapter uses the Rubric for Culturally Proficient Professional Learning to connect standards with practice.

8 Valuing Diversity

*Developing Skillful Leaders
to Create Support Systems for
Professional Learning*

*While informal interactions keep teachers connected, they are not
enough to support sustained, professional collaboration. For successful
collaboration—especially with the CCSS in mind—formal structures
and procedures must be developed, implemented, and maintained.*

—Dove & Honigsfeld, 2013, p. 176

GETTING CENTERED

As you read the quote from Dove and Honigsfeld (2013), what support
systems come to mind for professional learning at your school? Does
your school community demonstrate a value for diversity? In what ways
are structures as support systems for all students succeeding valued at
your school?

_____

_____

_____

_____

VALUING DIVERSITY BY CREATING SUPPORT SYSTEMS

The purpose of this chapter is to illustrate the importance of holding and demonstrating a high value for diversity in our schools and communities. Skillful leaders are mindful about creating and developing leadership capacity, a collaborative and trusting environment, and support systems for professional learning focused on improving educator practice that ensures all students are performing at high levels. These support systems include both internal and external networks. Internal networks include a districtwide professional learning plan that provides a shared understanding of the vision, outcomes, responsibilities, resources, and timelines for full implementation of a plan focused on the Common Core Standards. The commitment to a shared professional plan means you and your colleagues value diverse perspectives and are willing to share ideas and resources to improve schoolwide practices focused on student achievement. A professional learning plan built on student achievement data and outcomes allows you to hold yourself and your peers accountable for connecting your instructional practice to student achievement goals.

External networks might begin with an invitation to diverse partners, inside and outside the school community, to collaborate with math and English language arts faculty to design lessons and materials aligned with grade-level standards so that students graduate well prepared for college and careers. Partners include, but are not limited to, local universities and community colleges, area technology centers, hospitals and health centers, visual and performing arts centers, museums, amusement parks, feeder schools, districtwide "vertical" teams, and grade-level teams.

Valuing diversity comes in a variety of opportunities. You and your colleagues must begin at your own school looking for ways to construct support systems that value and use the expertise within your own schools and community. Require and expect diversity that supports the application of differentiated instructional and support strategies required for each student to meet the expectations of the Common Core. New and more rigorous standards as found in the Common Core will require additional implementation time, resources, and instructional support structures for all students. Teachers and leaders can learn those new strategies and will need a collaborative learning community to provide support through coaching, data collection and analyses, lesson planning and refinement, shared resources, shared inquiry, and collective commitment to equitable access and outcomes for students.

Chapter 6 presented Table 6.1, a rubric that displays an individual or a school moving from precompetent to culturally competent to culturally proficient behaviors for professional learning using the 5 Essential Elements as intentional behaviors. Table 8.1 displays the actions specifically aligned with the Essential Element of *Valuing Diversity* integrated with developing skillful leaders to create support systems for professional learning.

MOVE TO ACTION

Table 8.1 displays the actions consistent with the Essential Element of Valuing Diversity integrated with developing skillful leaders to create support systems for professional learning. As you think of your practice and your school's context, culturally proficient professional learning activities may include, but are not limited to, the following:

- Design sessions on differentiated instruction strategies using rational for all students learning.
- Create lesson designs with specific student outcomes based on grade-level standards that incorporate students' assets.
- Work collaboratively to develop action plans for grade-level, standards-based units using instructional strategies designed to engage all learners.
- Develop co-teaching units to use instructional strategies for students with special needs.
- Engage English-learning students and their families in school activities to determine instructional strategies to meet their needs.
- Special educators and educators of English-learning students give professional learning presentations to engage general educators in using instructional strategies for all learners.
- Design book studies using professional learning materials for gap-closing strategies.

We offer two case stories as examples of actions that demonstrate high value for diversity within the school community. These values are directly related to student achievement.

First, Mrs. W's story is an example of the importance of valuing diversity in ways that develop professional learning in support of all learners achieving at high levels. The rubric describes actions toward building a Culturally Proficient Professional Learning Plan.

Table 8.1 Valuing Diversity by Developing Skillful Leaders to Create Support Systems for Professional Learning

Informed by the Guiding Principles of Cultural Proficiency			
Transformation for Equity: *Focus on "Our Practice"*			
Valuing Diversity	**Culturally Proficient Professional Learning**	**And . . .**	**And . . .**
embraces differences as contributors to the value of your environment; addresses cultural experiences and opportunities.	recognizes that educator diversity can extend professional knowledge and understanding of staff and student cultures and experiences that can help students make connections to learning and a variety of pathways to academic success.	encourages educators to work collaboratively to learn new instructional and cultural competency skills to increase the variety of approaches effective for students with a range of assets and needs to learn and thrive.	relies on educators' diverse cultures, experiences, and capabilities to develop and lead staff learning and application of differentiated instructional and support strategies required for each student to meet expectations of the Common Core.

CELL PHONES AND SPIRIT CLUB: SUPPORT FOR PROFESSIONAL LEARNING THAT VALUES DIVERSITY

After being principal at Rock Canyon Elementary School for more than 30 days, Mrs. Washington returns from nutrition supervision to find a very determined sixth grader, Ella, waiting for her. In Ella's hand was an agenda. Mrs. W, as she is called by students, faculty, and community members, had already been briefed by the teacher of the SPIRIT class to expect this visit. This young lady is a representative from a group formed over eight years ago in the district in response to racial tensions that led to fights and disruptions on the middle and high school campuses. District leadership at that time, thought that including "diversity and conflict resolution" classes in the curriculum could help ease tension in the district. The schoolwide curriculum for that course had been developed eight years ago and had not been revised or updated since then.

Mrs. W understands that members of the SPIRIT group are well aware of the reasons the class was formed and offered as part of the required curriculum at Rock Canyon. The course is to teach students to address specific concerns regarding the climate and relationships between and among students on campus. They are also taught how to influence policy and practice in ways to make the school a place where all students are comfortable and look forward to attending. The students are taught to:

- Communicate effectively and use conflict resolution techniques.
- Understand their own cultural identity and the role it might play in cross-cultural conflicts.
- Understand and communicate concerns of students of ALL groups on campus.
- Actively engage in potential solutions for concerns presented.
- Sustain a respectful dialogue with authority figures (e.g., talk with the principal to address concerns).
- Understand and practice effective facilitation, communication between and among students on campus as well as with teachers, parents, and members of the community.

Ella sat with Mrs. W in her office and presented her agenda. The SPIRIT teacher had helped Ella to prepare the agenda and how to facilitate the meeting. The items on the agenda were not at all surprising to Mrs. W: bathrooms needed to be cleaner, some students needed more help with school supplies, the cell phone policy needed to be revised, and food in the cafeteria needed to be improved. Ella also said the SPIRIT group needed to focus on the "good" parts about diversity, not just on "conflicts." Mrs. W was a bit concerned about the cell phone item Ella had included on her agenda. Mrs. W assured Ella she and the staff needed to work on the cleanliness of the school, increasing school supplies, and improving the cafeteria food. She also told Ella that the entire course needed to be revised and updated, especially as it related to celebrating and valuing cultures. The conversation then turned to cell phones:

Mrs. W   *Ella, tell me more about why cell phones are important to elementary students?*

Ella   *Well, we have a hard time understanding why we can't use our cell phones. I guess some of us use them to talk with friends, parents,* *and siblings, but some of us use them for school. I can take pictures of homework assignments and things I need to do.*

Mrs. W   *For your homework? I didn't realize that. Do some of your teachers let you use your cell phone for homework and projects?*

Ella   *Oh, uh, I don't want to get my teacher in trouble. But in one of my classes, we can use our phone to take pictures of objects for our projects, and we can Google things real quick if we want to. Of course, some kids don't have cell phones, and that makes it hard for them.*

Mrs. W   *OK, I see. Anything else about cell phones and the SPIRIT class? Or school, in general?*

Ella   *Sometimes it helps me to listen to music during my lunch time. Or, I could be trying to call my mom to pick me up after school because practice was cancelled. If I try to do any of these things, my phone could be confiscated. Some kids get searched more often than other kids. We talked in our class that we notice that the black kids get searched for phones more than the white kids. That's huge for us!*

And we see teachers using phones during nutrition and lunch, and it's not considered wrong. Why don't we have the right to use our phones too?

Mrs. W   *Ella, thank you so much for bringing these items to my attention. I can't promise that we will change the "no cell phones on campus" policy, but we do need to examine the SPIRIT course. I'll get a group of teachers and students together to review the current course outcomes aligned with the new Common Core Standards for English language arts. I think we can bump things up a notch or two for this course. You have proven to me that sixth graders can really think things through and present a compelling case for all students. Would you like to serve on the curriculum committee?*

Ella   *I'd really like that, Mrs. W. Thanks for asking!*

The following week, Mrs. W convened a volunteer SPIRIT curriculum committee of teachers before she included any students. She reviewed her conversation with Ella without betraying Ella's confidence. She asked the teachers if they were willing to examine some of the school policies as well.

Peter   *Remember, one of the reasons the district didn't want our kids to have cell phones was because they were used to start fights. I'm not so* *sure the fights happen because of phones. If people are going to fight they're going to fight. Didn't kids fight when you were in school?*

Mrs. W   *Yes, we would set up fights by telegraph. (laughter)*

Edith   *But, do we agree that it is not appropriate during class time?*

Peter   *Well, I don't agree totally. I'm the teacher who lets students take pictures of their notes, assignment, or diagrams they make. I just wish more students had access to phones.*

Mrs. W   *Good point. Teachers can always make a decision when it is an appropriate use in their class. But other than that, should the policy hold?*

Edith   *I only have one thing to say. I want to be able to communicate with my child at the middle school. I know the phone should be off during class time. That makes sense to me. I don't use my phone during class. However, during my break I think I should be free to look at my phone and check my messages—from my kids.*

Tomas   *Not all messages are dangerous. Sometimes a kid needs to know that her grandpa is going to pick her up. Or to be ready to leave right away because they have an appointment. Some parents just can't wait until 3:15 for them to see the message.*

Erin   *I really need to point out, to some parents of a DHH student or other special learning students, the phone is a basic communication tool for them. This current policy is way too strict.*

Mrs. W   *Ok, let's work together to put some support systems in place to "pilot" a revised policy. I'll contact the superintendent and let him know what we are doing and why. Now, let's continue talking about other changes we need to make to support students in this course so they are better prepared for Common Core thinking.*

This is a story of an elementary student group that had acquired the skills and ability to advocate for a position. The work of the curriculum committee continues. Mrs. W learned through this process that collaborative curriculum planning and professional learning can address racial tensions by demonstrating a value for diverse perspective.

REFLECTION

If cell phones are not an issue at your school, what might be a comparable issue that impacts student access? In what ways did Mrs. W develop support systems through valuing diversity? What might be some ways that you that you can support professional learning at your school through inclusion and equity? How might multiple perspectives enhance professional learning plans? Take a few minutes and write your responses here.

_____

_____

_____

_____

THE NEW PRINCIPAL: WHO NEEDS TO BE IN THE CONVERSATION?

The second case story is about a new principal's learning experience as she meets members of the school community. Stephanie demonstrates her values for diversity as she engages in a conversation consistent with the Essential Element of *Valuing Diversity* integrated with developing skillful leaders to create support systems for professional learning.

Once again, Carla had been asked by her principal to serve as the school-community liaison and lead the planning team for the annual Stakeholders' meeting at the beginning of the academic year. She invited her friend Michael Proudbear to be her co-chair this year and, much to her delight, he agreed. Michael was a member of the local Tribal Council and had served as a member of the school's parent-teacher organization for many years. He was also a professor of Native American Studies at the local university.

As Carla and Michael began planning for the Stakeholders' event, Michael asked Carla if the school leaders truly were interested in gathering input from the community or was the meeting just a matter of a compliance issue. Carla was stunned by the question, but not by Michael's straightforward approach. One of the reasons she invited him to serve on the committee was the respect he received from the entire school community. In response to Michael's question, Carla arranged a meeting for them with the newly appointed elementary school principal, Stephanie McFarland.

Carla	*Stephanie, thanks for meeting with Michael and me. I know this is a busy time for you. Welcome to our school and the community.*
Stephanie	*Thanks so much, Carla. And Michael, I'm delighted to meet you. While I was principal at Carter Elementary for the past five years, I heard so many good things about you from members of our Native community. I look forward to working with you and the university.*

Michael	*I am honored to meet you, Stephanie. The Tribal Council and the faculty at the Center for Native American Studies Center welcome you to our community. How may we work together on this new project?*
Stephanie	*Well, there's really nothing new about this project. We just need to invite some local parents and community members to come to a meeting and give us some input and feedback on how the school is doing and for us to tell folks how we will implement the new Common Core State Standards. The school didn't really have an implementation plan, so I've decided we need to jump in and get one started by involving the community. We just don't have a lot of time.*
Carla	*We've always involved our community in schoolwide decisions here, so the community will be ready to respond.*
Stephanie	*Except the CCSS is a bit different from other initiatives in the past. These are rigorous standards that will require the faculty to develop curriculum and assessments aligned with those standards. We will need to work on new instructional strategies, also. These are big changes, so we need to let the community know what's coming.*
Michael	*Stephanie, with much respect for your knowledge and experience, might I offer you some information about the context of this school and community?*
Stephanie	*Well, certainly, Michael. I'd be interested in what you have to say.*
Michael	*This is a community school. What that means is the school is "of the community"; the school faculty and staff show value for the Native children by accepting their culture as assets rather than seeing their culture as a disadvantage. Many of the teachers engage with the parents at the community center for parent conferences and workshops instead of expecting requiring the parents to come to the school. Our children and youth have certain traditions that are honored by the teachers. The students are not penalized by celebrating those traditions during school days. So, you see, these traditions are part of the context in which the school functions.*
Stephanie	*That is good information for me to know, Michael. I had already thought about having you come to the school as a guest speaker to talk about some of the tribal traditions, you know, just to align with the curriculum.*

Carla *I think what Michael is saying, Stephanie, is that while the university is a very willing partner of the school, we have parent experts right here in our school community who will serve as resources to our teachers and our students. We need to make sure all parents are active members of our planning team, not just one-time attendees for an input session from stakeholders. Our parents and our community partners give us diverse perspectives and experiences that will help us build a rigorous and differentiated curriculum required for each student to achieve at high levels expected by the Common Core Standards. We have a different way of looking at professional learning—more inclusive, more community and student focused. We want our professional learning to reflect the value we hold for our community. Does that make sense?*

Stephanie *Well, yes, certainly. I need to slow down a bit and listen to what you two have in mind for the planning phase. I'm just so excited to be in this school. I want to get off to a good start. You've helped me see a different way of viewing community support and partnerships.*

Michael *We have a lot of work to do. Our Center on campus already has numerous partners that I will introduce to you. Together we can focus on the needs of all students.*

This story embraces and values differences as assets that can make a community stronger. The participants in the conversation are each an expert in an area of meeting needs of adults who serve students. Collectively and collaboratively they can use a variety of approaches that are effective for students with a wide range of assets and needs. External support structures such as community parent organizations, university faculty, and stakeholder groups, combined with administrative support, can provide teachers opportunities to use diverse instructional strategies required for each student to meet expectations of the CCSS.

REFLECTION

As you reflect on the conversation among the three people, what are the assumptions held by each of these prior to this meeting? What might be some outcomes established by Carla and Michael for the first Stakeholders meeting? In what ways might Stephanie's leadership actions change as a result of this conversation? What actions might she take to create support systems for more effective culturally proficient professional learning? Use Table 8.1 to guide your reflections about the actions of the three people in this conversation.

_____

_____

_____

_____

GOING DEEPER

This chapter guided you to understand the dynamic of valuing diversity when viewed as an action step. We can certainly espouse that we hold a value for difference and diversity, but our students and our community members will know how we live that value through our actions. What are your deeply held values for diversity? In what ways do you demonstrate those values? How do your students and your colleagues know who you are? What are the espoused values of your school? Are those values reflected in the vision and mission statements? Are you who you say you are? What do the data show to be the true values of the faculty and staff at your school?

DIALOGIC ACTIVITY

With a group of your colleagues, continue to engage in a dialogue to reach shared understanding of a school culture _valuing diversity by developing skillful leaders who create support systems for professional learning_. Continue the dialogue throughout small learning communities in your school and district. Once shared understanding has been reached, what might be some resources, strategies, and structures that could be developed and activated to support all learners, with emphasis on _college and career readiness_? What might be some of the thoughts and actions of your colleagues as a result of these conversations? Write your responses below.

_____

_____

_____

_____

Chapter 9 introduces the Essential Element of *Managing the Dynamics of Difference by Creating and Sustaining Learning Communities.* You will see the importance of knowing that conflict is a natural part of people working together in organizations. How we deal with that conflict in a culturally proficient manner is called managing the dynamics of our diversity and differences. Diversity is not a problem to be solved. Diversity is. It's a strength and an asset on which the community can grow, develop, and rely.

9 Managing the Dynamics of Diversity

Creating and Sustaining Learning Communities

The new curriculum helps students build the kind of educational scaffolding that will serve them well in high school and college. This is important for all kids, but it's particularly important at high-poverty, historically underperforming urban schools such as the one where I teach.

—Andrew Vega, teacher (2013, p. A17)

GETTING CENTERED

Professional learning communities have existed well before the last decade's discovery of them. If you have been an educator for 10 years or more, you recognize that many grade-level teams in elementary schools and department meetings often functioned as learning teams. The recognition of professional learning communities (PLCs) has provided a formal structure for looking at how educators organize to engage in our own learning. Take a few moments and think about how your PLCs, either formal or informal groupings, directly address or avoid issues of equity. How does your group address issues of access to high-level curriculum for all students, overrepresentation of low-income and students of color in special education courses, or disproportionate representation of students of color being suspended or expelled? Please use the space below to record your thinking.

MANAGING THE DYNAMICS OF DIVERSITY THROUGH LEARNING COMMUNITIES

The purpose of this chapter is to describe opportunities for professional growth and learning through communities of practice and PLCs by understanding the Essential Element of managing the dynamics of diversity. Creating and sustaining learning communities involves person-to-person interactions that are committed to improving practice in ways that over time demonstrably impact student achievement. In this context, educator professional learning that increases educator effectiveness and results for all students occurs within learning communities committed to continuous improvement, collective responsibility, and goal alignment (California Department of Education, 2013),

CULTURE SHIFTS IN SCHOOLS

Ann Lieberman and Lynne Miller (2014) describe real-world school settings where many educators are often caught between two organizational cultures. One culture is the transactional, hierarchical culture that projects norms and values of compliance. In seeming contrast is the more democratic culture projected by professional learning communities that values shared responsibility, creativity, and risk taking. Transformative leaders are able to provide for the transactional needs of keeping schools open and running through navigating bureaucratic shoals and ensuring that daily processes such as bell schedules and lunch supervision work as designed. At the same time, these transformative leaders take a long-term view of professional learning that includes learning and practicing inquiry and dialogic processes that embrace the diverse cultural assets of the community being served by the school.

MANAGING THE DYNAMICS OF DIFFERENCE THROUGH CREATING AND SUSTAINING LEARNING COMMUNITIES

A misrepresentation of professional learning communities is the formation or convening of any working group or team. For instance, a grade-level team is not necessarily a PLC. A PLC focuses on the ongoing learning of the "community" or the collaborative group that is carefully and intentionally aligned with the learning needs of all students. To meet these needs, educators within the learning community must design and implement complex support systems to deliver the actions needed for all students to achieve at high levels. The work of the learning community is mindfully built around continuous improvement with clear outcomes in mind. Those outcomes are aligned with the mission and vision of the school (Hord & Roy, 2014). Put another way, when we as educators bring our minds to our actions, we deepen the intended results.

The professional learning community provides the environment and structures to manage the dynamics of differences. Communication strategies and problem-solving techniques are part of the cultural norms of the learning community. Members of the learning community learn how to navigate between the cultures of rule-based bureaucracies and collaborative, reflective, supportive student-centered environments. Community members seek ways for inclusion and resolution rather than exclusion and isolation. Culturally Proficient facilitation and leadership supports a teaching and learning environment that is open to multiple perspectives and flexibility as a resource for resolution. Often, conversations about race, ethnicity, faith, class, sexual orientation, and gender can be highly emotional and can cause miscommunication and mismanagement of the real issues around student needs and student performance. When you hold a high value for diverse perspectives and experiences, you are more flexible and able to assess the potential for conflict and develop the skills to manage the dynamics of differences in your classroom and school. Conflict is a very natural part of people coming together in a work and learning place. You cannot always control the issues causing the conflict, but you can help people develop and manage healthy response to the conflict (Lindsey, Karns, & Myatt, 2012).

Table 9.1 presents the Essential Element *Managing the Dynamics of Difference*, with particular emphasis on Cultural Precompetence, Cultural Competence, and Cultural Proficiency to illustrate constructive fusion of the Essential Element with prevalent learning standards. Table 9.1 is derived from the rubric presented in Chapter 6, Table 6.1, and builds on Tables 7.1 and 8.1.

Take a moment and, first, read the definition in the first cell—Essential Element, *Managing the Dynamics of Difference*. Now read the next three cells to the right. Notice the progression from precompetence, to competence, to proficiency. Take particular note of the mindful, intentional development on the part of the leaders at the school—practicing, using, and applying. Take a few minutes and study Table 9.1.

Table 9.1	Managing the Dynamics of Difference by Creating and Sustaining Learning Communities		
	Informed by the Guiding Principles of Cultural Proficiency **Transformation for Equity:** *Focus on "Our Practice"*		
	Cultural Precompetence	**Cultural Competence**	**Cultural Proficiency**
Dynamics of Difference reframes differences so diversity is not perceived as a problem to be solved; promotes models using inquiry, dialogue related to multiple perspectives, and issues arising from diversity.	**Culturally Proficient Professional Learning** identifies and/ or structures opportunities for educators to learn and practice inquiry and dialogue models that help them confidently address issues arising from multiple perspectives.	**And . . .** leads to the development of communities of practice, where educators use inquiry and dialogue models to reframe anticipated or current issues they are facing in implementing equitable practices to address CCSS expectations.	**And . . .** enables educators to find ways to provide students with a range of instructional approaches and supports that fit their diverse set of assets and needs and meet different student, family, and institutional expectations that every student graduates college and career ready.

What is your reaction to the illustrations in Table 9.1? To what extent does this confirm your understanding of professional learning communities? In what ways does the information in the table inform your understanding of this Essential Element, *Managing the Dynamics of Difference*? How might this information be useful to you at your school? Please use the space below to record your thoughts and questions.

_____

_____

_____

_____

We hope with the study of this part of the Cultural Proficiency Professional Learning Rubric that you view educator interactions to include effective communications skills, problem-solving skills, and conflict resolution skills. These skills are embedded in the Common Core Standards as they relate to students' academic development and are important for us in our continuous improvement and professional learning.

MOVE TO ACTION

Table 9.1 displays the actions consistent with the Essential Element of Managing the Dynamics of Diversity by creating and sustaining learning communities. As you think of your practice and your school's context, culturally proficient professional learning activities may include, but are not limited to, the following:

- Conduct workshops on developing "pausing and paraphrasing" communication skills as part of parent-teacher conferences.
- Design professional learning sessions that focus on teacher-student conflict management conversations.
- Use PLC structure to develop Norms for Collaboration for all meetings.
- Develop facilitation skills for group processes (decision-making, problem-solving, brainstorming, consensus-building, etc.).
- Engage community partners to share "cultural norms" of local organizations, universities, tribes, churches, and so on.
- Train teachers and leaders in instructional coaching skills and meditational skills (e.g., Cognitive Coaching and Adaptive Schools training).
- Use book studies in PLCs to learn new communication strategies for various cultural groups to address students' instructional needs.

JUST ANOTHER LETTER IN THE INBOX: ONE INTERACTION AT A TIME

Let's now go to Capital City High School and a conversation between the principal, Ms. Edwards, and the chairperson of the Mathematics Department, Ms. Quinones.

It is another hectic day at Capital City High School. For the principal, like most days, papers are overflowing in her inbox. Among the papers is a draft of a letter for parents. On top of the paper is a small sticky note that states, "Please sign, we need it right away. Thank you. Ms. Quinones, Department Chair." At first glance, it looks like a typical letter home. However, the very first line gives Ms. Edwards pause. Under the elaborate school letterhead, the message begins with the following words:

Dear Parents,

Your child has decided to take this course against the recommendation of the teachers and Math department of Capital City H.S. Your child will need to work extremely hard to keep up with the class. It is his or her responsibility to seek out assistance and tutoring. He or she will not be allowed to drop the class or to switch teachers midyear. Please have a serious discussion with your child about taking this course. The following are the requirements to receive a passing mark in Calculus . . . .

The language of the letter is of concern for Ms. Edwards. She is immediately aware that she needs to have a conversation with Ms. Quinones, and the conversation needs to be well planned. She's fully aware that Ms. Quinones is highly respected by her colleagues and the students of Capital City H.S. At the same time, there's an underlying message that could be considered discouraging to parents and students. Ms. Edwards also knows that the Math Department had an agreed-upon letter that was much more inviting to parents and inclusive of a wider range of students. Ms. Quinones' letter is much different. It's a delicate and scary conversation to have in the first two weeks of being at a new school, especially if you are the principal. Nonetheless, it's an interaction that must take place.

Ms. Edwards invites Ms. Quinones into her office for a discussion.

Ms. Edwards: *Ms. Quinones, you left this letter for me to sign. I appreciate your approach to informing parents of the rigor of your course and the work required to maintain and achieve a passing grade. But I have a few edits I would like to share with you.*

Ms. Quinones: *I'm rather surprised. I've used this letter for several years. The other principals I have worked for have not had an issue with this letter. I really want parents to* *understand the work it takes, and clearly state my expectations for their children. You will learn quickly here, the parents are very demanding. I have written this letter to make sure there is no confusion about what is required. I have learned if it is not made abundantly clear, they will try to argue for higher grades or to drop the class.*

Ms. Edwards: *Your letter is very well written. I can see you clearly delineate what you would like students to do. It also clearly states the type of preparation you require each day. My concern is not about the content of the letter but rather the tone. I want to make sure we convey the department's message in the most effective tone and manner we can. I would like to suggest the following opening.*

Dear Parents:

Congratulations! Your child has taken on the challenge of this rigorous math course. Please take this opportunity to review with your child the resources available to him or her to successfully complete this course.

I would also like the letter to clearly state where and when tutoring and assistance is available.

Ms. Quinones: *I understand; however, I think the letter is fine the way it is. Again, the prior principal had no problem with how this letter was written.*

Ms. Edwards: *I certainly would be more comfortable with signing the letter if we could make these edits. I realize you are relying on a letter you have used successfully in the past, but I was expecting your letter would more closely reflect the draft of the letter agreed upon by your department—seemingly your department does function well as a learning community. I appreciate your dedication to ensuring that your expectations are clear. I also want students to feel welcome to the class and to the challenge. Your reputation precedes you, and I support and value your work. But I also wish to ensure all communications from the school are perceived as positive and supportive of students' achievement. I want students* *to feel encouraged to take the course. The first opening would actually make me afraid to take the course.*

Miss Quinones: *Well, I guess so. Well, if that's the way you want the letter. It still states the same message. Hmmmmm, I guess I overlooked the draft we crafted as a department—the PLC work is still so new for me. Actually, this letter does sound better.*

Ms Edwards: *I agree. Thank you for incorporating my edits and using your learning communities' work.*

It was clear to Ms. Edwards the work that lay before her. Ms. Quinones is, indeed, a dedicated teacher. As Ms. Edwards would learn, she worked effectively with both struggling and high-achieving students. She was a demanding, well-prepared, and supportive instructor. The work ahead was not about criticizing Ms. Quinones; rather, it was assisting her to understand how her language, and approach, may actively discourage students who would like to take on a rigorous course *because* Ms. Quinones was teaching it. Ms. Edwards understood that this first interaction had two messages—appropriate messages to parents and reinforcing the fact that PLCs are a source of good work. Ms. Quinones was complying but still seemed to be hesitant about the approach. It was an indicator that the work of PLCs was work that would need continued guidance; a marker of work needed to be done, one interaction at a time.

REFLECTION

As you reflect on the case story, what is your reaction to the conversation between Ms. Edwards and Ms. Quinones? How might you have handled this situation if you were Ms. Edwards? If you were Ms. Quinones? Please use the space below to record your comments. In what ways does the story illustrate the Essential Element of Managing the Dynamics of Diversity while sustaining learning communities?

_____

_____

_____

_____

A PLC AT WORK: A PLACE
FOR MANAGING OUR DIFFERENCES

Kent Roberts had served as PLC facilitator for three years at the K–8 school, mainly because no one else would step forward to accept the leadership role. This year, he was determined that he could convince Loretta Padilla that she was the best person for the job. Kent and Loretta had been co-teaching for the past two years, and he knew she was one of the best teachers in the school. Once again, no one else wanted to be "co-teachers" in the true sense of the word when their principal, Erik Weaver, described the opportunity to the faculty. As an eighth-grade language arts teacher, Kent had always asked for special education students to be placed in his classrooms. He looked forward to opportunities to work with Loretta and other special educators. Now, since the beginning of this year, they were collaborators. They shared the same classroom, designed assessments and lessons together, and hosted parent conferences together. Using the CCSS, they were creating new learning strategies that engaged all learners in rigorous and complex reading and writing activities.

Erik, the principal, had asked Loretta and Kent to present their teaching model to the faculty. He asked other faculty members to consider using some of the instructional strategies that Loretta and Kent were using as the CCSS were being implemented. Following their presentation, faculty met in their PLCs and discussed how co-teaching and other pedagogical support were important for implementing the CCSS at each grade level.

Kent asked if anyone wanted to facilitate the discussion for the PLC since he and Loretta had given the presentation. No one came forward.

Cooper	*I don't have a problem with you facilitating, Kent. You've always been a fair guy—no matter what the topic (laughter).*
Yvonne	*I don't have a problem with you facilitating. What I have a problem with is you and Erik thinking that all our special ed kids can pass all the same tests that normal, I mean, uh, regular kids can. There is a reason they are called "special," you know. I don't mean to sound cruel, but that's the way it is.*
Rose	*My issue is not nearly that complicated. I've been teaching by myself for so many years, I don't think I can share my space. I'd have to learn how to do that, you know, teach with another person in my room all the time.*
Cooper	*I was thinking just the opposite, Rose, how nice it would be to have a partner to teach with. I'd have to learn how to do that, but*

> *I think I have some good ideas, especially for math, to help kids with the CCSS.*

Loretta *Don't forget that we have the support of the PLC, too. We can work on this together. We can get help from the district office; we can do our own research and find the best practices; and we can share what we are learning with each other. That's the benefit of a PLC, right?*

Kelly *That's true, Loretta. Good points. But, wait a minute. Let's back up. I want to respond to Yvonne's comments earlier. I think we need to think about our kids differently. We need to know more about our students, all of them, yes, even our "special" kids. Once we know more about who they are, we can better design our lessons and our strategies to meet their needs. We need to show that we value them and their families.*

Carlo *We've been here before, folks. This is the conversation we were having when we started our Culturally Proficient book studies in the fall. We need to connect the dots here. Remember our discussions about seeing our kids for the assets they bring rather than seeing them as problems or deficits.*

Isn't this what we should be talking about in our PLC? We're smart enough to figure this out together. We just need to find the strategies that work best to prepare all our kids for college and the careers they want to have. We value teaching and we value our community, so let's get this done together.

This case story illustrates the power of people working together through a structure that supports managing the dynamics of different perspectives and experiences in the PLC structure.

GOING DEEPER

As you reflect on the chapter, what key ideas emerge for you? What might be some other structures the teachers could use to support all learners? Who might provide additional support to the PLC as partners for professional learning and Culturally Proficient action planning? What questions are missing from the conversations that you or your colleagues might add? Use Table 9.1 to guide your reflection on the actions of the people in the case stories in this chapter. In what ways might managing the dynamics of diversity support all students achieving Common Core expectations?

_____

_____

_____

_____

DIALOGIC ACTIVITY

With a group of your colleagues, continue to engage in a dialogue to reach shared understanding of a school culture _managing the dynamics of diversity by creating and sustaining learning communities._ Continue the dialogue throughout small learning communities in your school and district. Once shared understanding has been reached, what might be some resources, strategies, and structures that could be developed and activated to support all learners, with an emphasis on _college and career readiness_?

_____

_____

_____

_____

Chapter 10 presents a case story illustrating the importance of _Adapting to Diversity_ by applying evidence-based approaches to actively engage educators in improving practice. The chapter uses the Rubric for Culturally Proficient Professional Learning to connect standards with practice.

10 Adapting to Diversity

Applying Evidence-Based Approaches to Actively Engage Educators in Improving Practice

Preparing for the Common Core is preparing students to take their place in the world. Cultural incompetency is the hurdle and constant practice that has held inequity in place.

—Delia Estrada, personal communication (February 7, 2014)

GETTING CENTERED

One of the authors of this book was leading a professional learning experience with high school faculty in Glendale, California, a few years ago. The topic of the day was the changing demographics of the community, thereby the students in the school. In less than a decade, the community had experienced rapid immigration of newcomers from Armenia and in-migration of Latino students from Los Angeles. The teachers and administrators were committed to addressing issues of rapid growth and demographic change, and during one of the sessions a teacher rose and made a profound observation: "I think part of the problem is that we are still trying to teach the students who used to go here. It may be that we need to do things differently." All in attendance, including those leading the session, paused in stunned silence. We all slowly came to the awareness that our colleague was, indeed, correct.

As you read about the experience in Glendale, what is your reaction? Have you observed or heard of similar comments about the cultures of students attending your school? To what extent has your school experienced demographic changes in the last decade? Maybe your community has been stable. If so, in what ways has consideration of disaggregating student achievement influenced comments about students and their cultures at your school? Please use the space below to record your thinking and any questions that may be surfacing for you.

_____

_____

_____

_____

ADAPTING TO DIVERSITY BY ENGAGING EDUCATORS TO IMPROVE PRACTICE

The purpose of this chapter is to illustrate the dynamic of adapting to the diversity of the school community by engaging educators to improve their practice. Educators have made the point that our students today live in a fast-changing, complex, global, technological world. Educators must be prepared to adapt to the changing needs of our students and the communities they represent.

Adopting the Common Core State Standards (CCSS) or similar other state-level initiatives involves instructional changes, educators' exposure to a wide variety of cultural perspectives, and collective action by educators and the communities they serve to support a wide variety of instructional approaches. Culturally relevant pedagogy and instruction is not new and has, in fact, been in place for some time (Gay, 2000; Ladson-Billings, 1994). The effectiveness of culturally relevant pedagogy related to the ability of educators and their schools to authentically engage in the "inside-out" process resonates throughout this book. As educators, we are to look deep inside to assess our values and behaviors toward and about the cultures of our students and their families—racial, ethnic, socioeconomic, sexual orientation, faith, and special abilities, among others. Once we are clear on being willing and able to educate all children because of their cultural membership and not in spite of their cultures, then we are well prepared to examine the policies and practices of the school and district that either impede or facilitate quality instruction.

It is important to understand that individual change on the part of educators versus systemic change on part of the school or district is not an *either-or* dynamic; it is a *both-and* dynamic. The Common Core State Standards, used appropriately, provide the opportunity to adapt to who our students are, not who they used to be or who we might like them to be. Change begins with ourselves as educators and simultaneously with the schools that employ us.

Anne Gregory, James Bell, and Mica Pollock (2014) summarized the types of opportunities available as we adapt to who our students are through providing supportive relationships, offering academic rigor, offering cultural relevancy and responsiveness in instruction and inter-actions with students, and establishing bias-free classrooms and respect-ful school environments. Adapting our practices and polices to serving diverse student communities results in educators' exposure to a wide variety of demographic groups' perspectives—race, ethnicity, socioeco-nomic, and sexual minorities, among others.

Table 10.1 portrays the Essential Element *Adapting to Diversity*, with particular emphasis on Cultural Precompetence, Cultural Competence, and Cultural Proficiency to illustrate constructive fusion of the Essential Element with prevalent learning standards. Table 10.1 is derived from the rubric presented in Chapter 6, Table 6.1, and builds on Tables 7.1, 8.1, and 9.1.

Take a moment and, first, read the definition in the first cell—Essential Element, *Adapting to Diversity*. Then, read the next three cells to the right. Notice the progression from precompetence, to competence, to profi-ciency. Take particular note of the mindful, intentional development on the part of the leaders at the school—practicing, using, and applying. Take a few minutes and study Table 10.1, and look to the action words of "doing."

MOVE TO ACTION

Table 10.1 displays the actions consistent with the Essential Element of *adapting to diversity by applying evidence-based approaches to actively engage educators in improving practice.* As you think of your practice and your school's context, culturally proficient professional learning activities may include, but are not limited to, the following:

| **Table 10.1** | Adapting to Diversity by Applying Evidence-Based Approaches to Actively Engage Educators in Improving Practice | | |

	Informed by the Guiding Principles of Cultural Proficiency **Transformation for Equity:** *Focus on "Our Practice"*		
	Cultural Precompetence	**Cultural Competence**	**Cultural Proficiency**
Adapting to Diversity teaches and learns about differences and how to respond to them effectively; facilitates change to meet the needs of the community.	**Culturally Proficient Professional Learning** helps educators develop understanding about instructional changes required by the new Common Core Standards, determine current capacities and needs to implement equity-focused policies and practices, and initiate ongoing educator learning and support to develop expertise and confidence.	**And . . .** extends educator experiences related to a variety of equity perspectives, including race, gender, language, sexual orientation, religion, special abilities and needs, and socioeconomic status that may impact students' initial ability to meet CCSS expectations.	**And . . .** promotes collective action to develop and apply policies and practices that support the wide variety of instruction and support services required by diverse students engaged in meeting CCSS standards and moving toward college and careers.

- Develop Common Core committees charged with examining the grade-level standards and expected outcomes aligned with student performance for all demographic groups. Develop "gap-closing" professional learning plans to address student needs.
- Work collaboratively with parents and community members to understand and implement Common Core Standards.
- Create "research teams" to explore "best practices" being used in schools with similar context and student demographic groups.
- Explore regional, county, state, and federal resources available to support implementation specific to school needs.
- Find and invite new community partners as guest presenters to help with adapting to changing demographics of school community. Invite new members to serve on school committees.

- Develop workshops on assessing the school and student needs based on student performance on Common Core assessments as well as multiple assessments.
- Understand the importance of "adapting to diversity" through professional learning experiences designed with teachers, staff members, and administrators.

REFLECTION

When reading Table 10.1 and the list of culturally proficient professional learning activities, what thoughts or reactions occur to you? To what extent does this confirm your understanding of improving practice? In what ways does the information in the table inform your understanding of this Essential Element, *Adapting to Diversity*? How might this information be useful to you at your school? What activities might you add to the list? Please use the space below to record your thoughts and questions.

_____

_____

_____

_____

THE EMPRESS OF HOULTVILLE

Miss Hoult became well known to Lupe (Ms. E) early on. Feisty and dedicated she introduced herself, jokingly, to Ms. E. as the Empress of Houltville, as that is how her students know her. She stated, "I am the Empress of my classroom, and no one lays down the law in my classroom but me." Of course, she explains, it is a benevolent dictatorship. One of the co-department chairs for English, she is dedicated to providing rigorous instruction to all her students. One of the founders of the Humanities program, she's always willing to explore and refine her craft. When students speak of Miss Hoult, they smile and say she's funny, serious, and knows what she wants in an essay.

One day Ms. E's district supervisor, Dr. Ocampo, paid her a visit. Like a good instructional leader, Lupe insisted they do informal observations. The classroom visits were unannounced and impromptu. As they entered Miss Hoult's class, the students were energetically discussing and debating a point of grammar. Miss Hoult was engaged in a warm-up activity where students had to identify and correct grammatical errors in the text presented. Miss Hoult was using the DocuCam video and screen so all students were engaged in the reading and editing process.

Miss Hoult	*So tell me what you see? Is it correct? Or does it need a little work?*
Allan	*Look i's right there, 'the' should be right in front of the name. It changes the whole meaning of the sentence if 'the' is not in the right place.*
Beth	*I see something else, the first word should be capitalized.*
Miss Hoult	*Those are two very good observations. Does everyone agree? Are we done editing this piece? Is there anything else? (Students murmur their agreement. One student, near the back sits straight up.) Byron does not think we are done!*

A young English-learning student, fidgety and restless, has nonetheless been following the discussion. As he sits up, Byron proudly and loudly declares his disagreement with the group.

Byron	*Nope! We are not done. I think I see one more.*
Miss Hoult	*Byron, tell us your astute observation.*

Byron seems to pause, he seems unsure of himself after his initial proclamation. All the students are watching him. He is silent but continues to fidget. Miss Hoult waits for one minute. The class begins to grow restless.

Miss Hoult	*Everyone hold on. Byron is thinking out his answer. See if you can find what he found. Always take the time to think. Give him time. Give him time.*

The teacher waits another minute. Byron shuffles in his seat. But it is also obvious he's intently analyzing the example on the screen.

Miss Hoult	*Good. Take your time with your thinking. Byron, would you like to check your thinking with the partner of your choice?*
Byron	*I want to figure this out on my own.*

Miss Hoult	*Okay everyone. Can you see what Byron sees? Discuss it in pairs.*

Miss Hoult	*No, don't shout out. Byron is figuring it out; we are giving him space to think.*

Miss Hoult waits.

Byron	*I think I do need to put this word before that word. It's not really a mistake, but I think it makes it sound better.*

Students murmur appreciation.

Miss Hoult	*Listen to what Byron said! He's thinking like a writer! He took the time to think of the sentence as a whole. We were talking about editing, but he taught us how to make a sentence better. He was thinking like a writer. Well done, Byron! Let's give him a hand.*

The class applauds.

Later in a follow-up conversation with Lupe and Dr. Ocampo, Miss Hoult admits needing to work specifically on her approach with Byron. She realizes he can be easily bored. He has been known to interrupt class with some of his comments. He can derail a class. However, she appreciates his wit and quick intelligence.

Miss Hoult	*I just need to channel that energy. He is very bright, but he also needs the class to appreciate how smart he really is. Not just as a clown, but as a scholar, as a writer, as a thinker. Today was a wonderful opportunity. I jumped on board. It was a risk I was willing to take. But I also had to orchestrate an honorable way out. I'm so glad he met the challenge. I have a confession to make. Byron can drive me nuts. I have to tell you the truth; there wasn't another error. I had to ride it, mainly as he was so involved in this mini lesson. It was a golden moment. I wanted to accentuate what he could bring to the class. It would be way too easy for all our interactions to be about what he wasn't doing. However, he was with me. He was in the lesson. You are right, it was a good moment. I know this 'wait-time' stuff we are focusing on in our professional learning is working*

for our EL students—well, for all our students. This means all students can work on reaching Common Core thinking if we do our job.

Lupe   *Dr. Ocampo, I always enjoy stopping by Miss Hoult's class. She engages students in ways that they feel included.*

Dr. Ocampo   *Yes, I could see that. Seems this focus on Cultural Proficiency and implementing the Common Core Standards are working well together.*

REFLECTION

As you reflect on the setting and the conversation above, what are some things that emerge for you? In what ways was Miss Hoult using the Essential Element of *Adapting to Diversity* to improve her practice? What role might Dr. Ocampo play in working with Lupe to improve schoolwide instructional practice?

IMPROVING OUR PRACTICE THROUGH THE COMMON CORE

The CCSS has presented us with the opportunity for educators to focus on specific expectations for all learners. Those expectations will be achieved through classroom instruction that is aligned with and focused on curriculum and grade-level skills. As educators we know that not all students gain academic knowledge and skills in the same way. We also know they bring different life experiences, learning experiences, and language development experiences. The CCSS offers the perfect time for educators to provide diverse learners *access to rigorous curriculum and high-quality instruction* (Dove & Honigsfeld, 2013, p. 8).

The following case story is an illustration of how adapting to the diversity of our students and the willingness to improve our practice can lead to improved student achievement.

Ginger and Claudia discussed their plans on their way to their professional learning community meeting. Today is Ginger's turn to bring a problem of practice to the PLC and she is eager, slightly embarrassed, and happy to have Claudia as her partner for support. While Claudia and she had talked a lot about the challenge, they were a little short on what to do or how to begin to address it. Ginger and Claudia are both English language arts teachers at Central View Middle School. Their principal, Lupe Estrada, has led the faculty in creating PLCs and using the lens of Cultural Proficiency as their professional development focus for the year to help implement the new CCSS. Claudia and Ginger have teamed with their social studies partners to develop grade-level units and materials. They are most proud of the unit called *Who Am I?*

Claudia *I can't believe we didn't recognize this earlier. This seemed like the perfect assignment to match the unit objectives.*

Ginger *I know. We were trying so hard to make the unit meaningful to our kids . . . and then we missed the mark.*

The PLC meeting started. Hiram, the school counselor and the PLC facilitator, introduced Ginger and Claudia and invited them to describe their problem of practice to PLC members.

Ginger *Claudia and I started our 'Who Am I?' unit last year as an opener for our seventh-grade English Language Arts program. In it, we get to know students by asking them to write their autobiographies. It seemed to go well last year. So, we tried it again this year. We give them miniassignments like bringing baby pictures to put on the bulletin board or interviewing their grandparents about what they did as teenagers or developing a family tree or taking a short personality test and writing about the results. Although it seemed to go well last year, Claudia and I are a bit worried. After our parents' night meeting, we had some concerns expressed. Mrs. Mohammed questioned me about how much private information Jeron would have to share to get a good grade.*

Claudia *Then, later, Mr. and Mrs. Jackson flatly stated that their boys wouldn't be writing about the family and explained that, as foster parents, they were cautious about their boys' feelings about difficult family situations that had placed them in foster care. The Jacksons offered that the boys would make up work or do an alternate assignment, but that family history wasn't something they believed we could handle well as a common or just-for-fun assignment. Rodrigo Sanchez, a student from my class last year, stopped me on my way out and said he didn't want his little brother to have to do the presentation in front of the class because he was worried about classmates teasing him about his accent. I thanked them for their comments and said my co-teacher and I would be considering all of this information as we finished planning the unit.*

Ginger	*So, after thinking about our options, Claudia and I decided to ask you to help us redesign our unit. This is a great opportunity for us to transform this unit into one that integrates our new Common Core expectations and what we've been learning about in our Cultural Proficiency workshops. Clearly we need to make changes. We still want to focus on the lives of our students, to personalize their learning, but certainly more thoughtfully . . . .*
Claudia	*And . . . Hiram, we can make our professional learning community time really work for us. As PLC members, you can help us draft our reading and writing assignments, and we can include themes from your World Civilization class, Oscar, and maybe some ideas from math or science, Judy and Simon, and then . . . .*
Ginger	*And . . . as you can see, we really need your help!*
Hiram	*I know I'm the academic counselor and not a teacher, but I see this as a great opportunity for us to try out some of the professional development we've experienced by putting together—and trying out—a solid unit, even a culturally proficient unit. The Who Am I? theme is really something that fits all of us who are teaching and supporting our kids.*
Oscar	*And, it's a good theme for us, as well. "Who am I, and who do I need to be to help you?" I'm in. Who else?*
Judy	*I'm not certain how math fits into this theme, but I'm willing to try. How do we get started?*

As the other PLC members agreed to commit PLC time for the next three sessions to this problem of practice, they started laying out the expectations and outcomes for the unit.

At the next session, Ginger unfurled three charts she and Claudia had drafted: (1) Common Core Objective(s), (2) Possible Reading and Writing Assignments, (3) Cautions and Options.

Hiram	*What does chart three mean?*
Ginger	*Claudia and I want to make sure to look at possible bias and insensitivities in the reading and writing assignments. From the beginning, we want to attend to the comments we received on Parents' Night and draft the new unit with alternative books and writing prompts to ensure that every student can fully participate in studying, reading, and writing about themselves and others.*

Oscar   *Ok, then, I think we need a few more charts. Let's think about this unit through the lens of Cultural Proficiency. Let's decide what Essential Element from our Cultural Proficiency work we are addressing. And let's identify our own professional learning goals for this work.*

Judy   *Yes, what do we as professional educators need to know and do to make sure our students learn about themselves—whoever they are and wherever they come from?*

Ginger   *I'll add a chart titled "Essential Element—Adapting to Diversity." We'll make copies of that element from the Cultural Proficiency/ Professional Learning rubric we reviewed in the summer institute to use as a reference for what we should be doing to move from precompetence to proficient.*

Claudia   *These are pretty good parameters for our work together. Let's put up a couple of initial ideas to think about so we'll be ready to actually start developing the unit at next week's meeting.*

As the team began to brainstorm ideas, Claudia and Ginger captured the ideas on the charts:

- Common Core Objectives—English Language Arts Standards, Grades 6–8
- Literature: Stories—adventure stories, myths, historical fiction; Poetry—narrative poems, ballads, epics; Literary nonfiction—personal essays, speeches, biographies, memoirs; Check with district librarian to provide reading lists and materials.
- Writing ideas: Write a narrative to develop a real or imagined experience or events using well-chosen details and well-structured sequences.
- Informational text: Compare and contrast one author's presentation of events with that of another, for example a memoir written by the subject and a biography of the same subject written by another author.
- History/Social Studies: Distinguish among fact, opinion, and reasoned judgment in a text.

Oscar   *This is good. This last one is what this problem of practice is trying to address. We should be doing this kind of planning for all of our lessons.*

Claudia   *Thank you so much for your time today and all of your ideas on ways for us to extend our teaching to reach all of our students.*

Ginger   *I'll follow up with Marina, the librarian. And, Oscar, can we talk about your social studies plans to see where we might connect? The standards make it so clear that these are the years when early adolescents learn about themselves and about people whose experiences and backgrounds are different.*

And with that, the PLC adjourned until the next week with a clear agenda for their future work.

REFLECTION

In what ways is this case story an example of *adapting to diversity by improving our practice*? What emerged for you as an educator as you read about Claudia and Ginger? What might be some things that you learned about yourself as you read this case story? In what ways did Oscar and Hiram improve their practice? What's missing from this story?

GOING DEEPER

Think about the dynamic of *adapting*. Now that you have read this chapter and thought about the complexity of schooling in this era, what thoughts and feelings emerge for you? What do you view in your current setting as challenges? What strengths and assets do you bring to your school? What are you learning from these case stories that inform the application of evidenced-based approaches to improving educator's practice through the lens of adapting to diversity? What is there about the community you serve that you would like to learn? Please take a few moments and use the space below to jot your thinking, or maybe draw a picture.

_____

_____

_____

_____

DIALOGIC ACTIVITY

With a group of your colleagues, continue to engage in a dialogue to reach shared understanding of a school culture *adapting to diversity by applying evidence-based approaches to actively engage educators in improving practice*. We invite you to explore with colleagues ways you want support, becoming increasingly effective in providing supportive relationships, offering academic rigor, offering cultural relevancy and responsiveness in instruction and interactions with students, and establishing bias-free classrooms and respectful school environments.

_____

_____

_____

_____

Chapter 11 presents a case story illustrating the importance of *institutionalizing cultural knowledge by applying and connecting a common commitment toward common outcomes for all students*. A school principal works with teachers to design curriculum that is aligned with Common Core Standards. The chapter uses the Rubric for Culturally Proficient Professional Learning to connect standards with practice.

11 Institutionalizing Cultural Knowledge

Applying and Connecting a Commitment Toward Common Outcomes for All Students

My concern is not to deny the political and directive nature of education —a denial that, for that matter, it would be impossible to reduce to act— but to accept that this is its nature, and to live a life of full consistency between my democratic option and my educational option, which is likewise democratic.

—Paulo Freire, 1998, p. 79

GETTING CENTERED

In reading this far with us, you now know our primary interest is providing equitable access and opportunities to all students with the Common Core State Standards (CCSS) serving as the current promise or vehicle to that end. This is a journey we begin as individual educators through continuing to learn in ways that inform our practice, whether as teachers, counselors, or administrators. Then, as we collaborate with our colleagues, we initiate and sustain policies and practices to institutionalize theories and principles of equity designed to ensure our high school graduates are college and career ready. As you think about the next year or two in your career and with your current school or district assignment, what might be some things you would set as goals for your learning? Your goals might be for your own pedagogy, or they might include what you would like to learn about the community you serve. Similarly, what might be some topics of professional learning you recommend for your school or district? Think about your responses and use the space below to record your thinking.

_____

_____

_____

_____

INSTITUTIONALIZING CULTURAL KNOWLEDGE TOWARD COMMON OUTCOMES

The purpose of this chapter is to present the Essential Element of *Institutionalizing Cultural Knowledge* and how that knowledge moves a school toward common outcomes for all students. This Essential Element combines with the other four elements in Chapters 7 to 10 interdependently to roll out individual and school-based approaches to professional learning. Chapter 12 provides a template for documenting your new knowledge findings, your lines of inquiry, and your plan of action. In preparation for that level of thinking and planning, it is useful to consider what it is you know and what you need to know and to learn. Being an *inside-out* approach, Cultural Proficiency by its very nature is focused on applying principles of reflection to our own continuous growth and to our school's continuous improvement.

Learn theories and principles of equity. Culturally proficient teachers, counselors, and administrators are involved with their own learning. Culturally proficient teachers learn and use instructional approaches such as scaffolding and research-based strategies to ensure that their students make demonstrated progress toward standards. Such instruction is focused on student mastery as the end result, not for the school's performance on standardized tests. Quality professional learning is focused on supporting educators who know and understand issues of equity and access as they relate to student outcomes. Effective teachers need support from their site and district administrators to help create and maintain conditions supportive of all students learning.

Individual and collective learning. Counselors and administrators view their primary responsibility as supporting teachers' effective classroom instruction. They focus on working with teachers to identify and mitigate barriers to student learning and access. Such barriers might be current policies and practices that limit student access. For example, pervasive year-over-year low reading or mathematics achievement, professional learning that rarely focuses on instruction, or limited knowledge about the impact of changing demographics of the community get in the way of teachers doing their best work.

Generally speaking, educators view professional learning as a fundamental part of their day-to-day activities. Educators continuously reflect on practice as individuals, both in informal times with colleagues and during formal meeting opportunities. Grade-level meetings, department meetings, all-school meetings, professional learning sessions, and meetings with parent-community members are characterized with learning as their central purposes.

Assess policies and practices. Culturally proficient educators recognize that all policies and practices were developed at some point in time to serve very specific purposes and outcomes. As such, these educators continuously examine the assumptions underlying prevalent practices to ensure they still serve the needs for which they were initially designed. When the review of student data reveals areas of student academic needs, culturally proficient leaders take these data as a signal that current policy or practice may need to be revised or replaced to better serve the access and academic needs of students. The constant focus in this environment is to determine student needs and to make decisions that best serve their needs.

Results in students being college and career ready. Culturally proficient educators view themselves as professional learners continuously evolving their theory of instruction (i.e., pedagogy). Such educators view the students in their classrooms and schools as instruments for indicating the success and areas of improvement needed in their professional practice. Similarly, culturally proficient educators collaborate with colleagues to keep a common goal in mind—their students becoming college and career ready. Whether one is working in a preschool or a high school, culturally proficient educators recognize their roles in student development. The Common Core Standards provide grade-level standards that hold all educators responsible to prepare learners to be ready for the next level, culminating with high school exit standards for college and career readiness.

CULTURALLY PROFICIENT PROFESSIONAL LEARNING—INSTITUTIONALIZING CULTURAL KNOWLEDGE TOWARD COMMON OUTCOMES

Table 11.1 portrays the Essential Element *Institutionalizing Cultural Knowledge*, with particular emphasis on Cultural Precompetence, Cultural Competence, and Cultural Proficiency to illustrate constructive fusion of the Essential Element with *Applying and Connecting a Common Commitment Toward Common Outcomes for All Students*. Table 11.1 is derived from the rubric presented in Chapter 6, Table 6.1, and builds on Tables 7.1, 8.1, 9.1, and 10.1.

First, read the definition in the first cell—Essential Element, Institutionalizing Cultural Knowledge. Then, read the next three cells to the right. Notice the progression from precompetence, to competence, to proficiency. Take particular note of the purposeful development on the part of the leaders at the school—practicing, using, and applying. Take a few minutes and study Table 11.1, with careful attention to the action words of "doing."

MOVE TO ACTION

Table 11.1 displays the actions consistent with the Essential Element of *institutionalizing cultural knowledge by applying and connecting a commitment toward common outcomes for all students.* As you think of your practice and your school's context, culturally proficient professional learning activities may include, but are not limited to, the following:

- The districtwide commitment to equitable outcomes for all demographic student groups is demonstrated through high-quality professional learning for all educators. The question for commitment becomes: *Do we believe we can educate all learners?*
- The district and schools create an ongoing, systematic action plan that develops structures, resource, timelines, and materials for professional learning that improves educators' practice specifically focused on the implementation of the CCSS.

Table 11.1 Institutionalizing Cultural Knowledge Toward Common Outcomes

	Informed by the Guiding Principles of Cultural Proficiency Transformation for Equity: *Focus on "Our Practice"*		
	Cultural Precompetence	**Cultural Competence**	**Cultural Proficiency**
Institutionalizing Cultural Knowledge changes systems to ensure healthy and effective responses to diversity; shapes policies and practices that meet the needs of a diverse community.	**Culturally Proficient Professional Learning** provides the means for educators to learn about and practice theories and principles of equity that can support or hinder culturally responsive policies and actions related to student learning success.	**And . . .** promotes educators' developing the structure and processes for an ongoing, comprehensive system of individual and collective learning that responds to diverse and changing educator and student needs with reliable supports to meet CCSS expectations that every student graduates ready to be successful in college or a career.	**And . . .** includes educators' reviewing individual and collective professional learning experiences and results over time to evaluate whether professional learning efforts and changes in policies and practices are having an impact on educator effectiveness and, ultimately, all students' performance and well-being.

- District and site administrators receive professional development to support their communities of practice as leaders of the implementation of equity-based CCSS.
- Engage faculty in professional learning focused on review of policies and practices that impact student outcomes and equity and access issues (e.g., student grading policies, discipline policies, special education placement, honors and advanced placement).

- Publish and make public policy chances (institutionalize) resulting from inequity of outcomes, disproportionalities of student discipline and class placements, and lack of access to resources discovered during data collection and analyses sessions.

REFLECTION

When reading Table 11.1 and the activities described above, what questions, thoughts or reactions occur to you? In what ways does this support your understanding of Culturally Proficient Professional Learning? In what ways does the information in the table inform your understanding of this Essential Element, *Institutionalizing Cultural Knowledge*? How might this information be useful to you at your school? What activities might you add to the list? Please use the space below to record your thoughts and questions.

_____

_____

_____

_____

OPPORTUNITY PRECEDES ACHIEVEMENT

Three years ago, Middletown USD's Chief Academic Officer, Veronica Bays-Jackson, had convened a committee comprised of the high school principal, the school counselors, and members of the English language arts and mathematics departments. This year, she asked Lupe Estrada, principal of the middle school, and two middle school teachers to join the committee. As a career-long supporter of equity issues, Veronica knew that Lupe had made inroads at the middle school toward implementing the CCSS using the lens of Cultural Proficiency. Veronica was well aware of the many faces of resistance that can be manifest in schools, and she viewed the Common Core State Standards as an excellent opportunity to fuse equity and excellence.

The committee met for a week during the summer to begin a process of confronting academic inequities revealed in the disaggregated high school achievement data. The theme for this professional learning was to internalize the Tools of Cultural Proficiency in ways that would make higher level English and mathematics courses open to all students. Committee members spent three days learning the Tools of Cultural Proficiency, which entailed deep reflection to explore and understand how assumptions about culture influence in often unseen and unrecognized ways their beliefs about students' capacity and ability for higher order thinking.

The final two days of the weeklong professional learning involved applying the Tools of Cultural Proficiency to policies and practices at Capital City High School that created and maintained some courses that had enrolled very few students of color. With the aid of district office computer analysts, the committee members learned that sections of English and mathematics were stratified by race, ethnicity, and socioeconomics. The initial dialogue sessions were a difficult learning process met with acrimony and expressions of feeling "blamed." Dr. Bays-Jackson skillfully navigated the dialogue sessions in ways that provided for personal expressions and opportunities for participants to learn others' viewpoints. The result was an acknowledgment that, yes, the de facto tracking at the school was a poorly kept secret and, yes, teachers did vie to teach the "good kids" and strive not to have to teach "those poor unfortunate, though, struggling kids."

It had taken about two years for the principal, the counselors, and the teachers to fully de-track the English courses. Progress with the math department was slower, but with benefits. One of the outcomes for the math faculty was to learn of the need to more intentionally develop a cohesive, vertically aligned curriculum that ensured appropriate math competencies for teachers and administrators, PK–8. Response from the English department faculty was decidedly mixed in the first year and became increasingly supportive in the second year as faculty began to see value in learning culturally relevant instructional strategies aligned with the CCSS.

To some surprise, several students were initially resistant. Many expressed that either they were not smart enough for the "advanced classes" or they were intimidated by being in classes with "those smart kids." Some students expressed concerns that the teachers were too hard and wouldn't help them in the advanced classes. The counselors and principals had to prevail with several students to give it a try for at least a year. By the end of that first year, student resistance began to wane.

By the end of the second year, disaggregated student assessment data for English language arts began to indicate a narrowing of achievement scores. Gains were not stellar or over the top, but notable progress was being made. However, this new awareness of how to use disaggregated data led to surfacing new questions. These new questions were about the demographic profiles of suspended and expelled students.

OPPORTUNITY AND DISPROPORTIONALITY

At the request of the teachers and principal at Capital City High School, Dr. Bays-Jackson provided another weeklong professional learning opportunity in the summer following the second year of implementation. The theme for the week was *Opportunity Precedes Achievement.* The first day was a refresher with the Tools of Cultural Proficiency as applied to data analysis using the book *Culturally Proficient Inquiry* (Lindsey, Graham, Westphal, & Jew, 2008). The balance of the week was devoted to in-depth study of disproportionality. Data were provided that showed racial, ethnic, socioeconomic, and gender profiles for students in special education, students assigned to in-school suspension, out-of-school suspensions, and expulsions. Lupe and her teachers brought their school data for review, as well.

On Wednesday the professional learning group was divided into teams to review data and to look for themes and anomalies. In this small group are the high school principal, Ms. Lopez, two English teachers, Sally and Edward, a counselor, Freda, and Lupe, principal at the middle school.

Edward	*I am stunned by these data! Am I reading this correctly? Are African American males actually suspended at a rate 140% in excess of their proportion of the student population? As a teacher, I find this frightening.*
Sally	*You are kidding, aren't you? Have you noticed that group that hangs out in the quad at lunchtime? They just look like gangbanger troublemakers!*
Ms. Lopez	*Well, we certainly have two different perspectives here, don't we? It would be helpful to me if each of you would share why you believe as you do? Edward, what is it about the data you find upsetting, and, Sally, how do you jump to use of the term "gangbangers"?*
Edward	*For me, I am stunned that so many students are suspended. I guess I live in my little cocoon, because I can't recall the last time I sent anyone to the office to be disciplined. However, what I find frightening about these data is it makes the school look really bad. Up until we started this open enrollment process for our English courses, I taught all levels of students and don't recall African American students being any more troublesome than any other students.*
	Sally, I am most troubled by your use of the term gangbangers. I must admit I find careless use of that term offensive and really want to hear your perspective.

Sally	*I'm really embarrassed! I don't know where that came from.*
Freda	*Sally, this is a good illustration of what we confronted on Monday with that session on Barriers to Cultural Proficiency. Until I took my counseling courses, I had not taken that "inside-out" look that we are not doing with Cultural Proficiency. Though you made the statement, this is about all of us and the extent to which we might stereotype kids.*
Ms. Lopez	*For me, this conversation is important at another level. We need to expand opportunities for this kind of introspection to the entire faculty and staff. As we end this week, I have asked the facilitator to reserve Friday afternoon for us to decide the next steps in going schoolwide with this work.*
Lupe	*We are having great success at our school with this same conversation.*
	Maybe it's time we took this work districtwide. You know, with resources from the district. This is important work if we are going to move forward with the Common Core.
Ms. Lopez	*You are right, Ms. Estrada. These data will support your point of view.*
Edward	*Good point, Ms. L. We still have today's task, which is to examine the data for themes and anomalies. Another theme I see is African American males are also overrepresented in special education courses.*
Sally	*You know, on Monday when the facilitator showed the slide titled **Opportunity Precedes Achievement,** I didn't make a clear connection to how that was going to relate to achievement data. Now his comment, "If the students are not in school or are locked in classes designed for low-ability students," resonates loudly. I can honestly say, I am not comfortable with this line of inquiry but I now see the need for it. With the conversations about Common Core, now is the perfect time to talk about high standards for all kids.*
Freda	*Yes, it is going to be a steep learning curve for all of us. It is a good thing we are educators—hopefully, learning is what we do well.*
Lupe	*This has been a helpful conversation for me in my personal and professional journey toward becoming a culturally proficient educator and principal. One thing I know we need to*

do at our schools and in the district is to make our work and our learning public. The facilitator asked us a hard question at the end of our professional development session last week. He asked: "Now that you know what you know, to what are you willing to commit?"

That means we can no longer ignore what we have known for a long time. We have to work together to make changes throughout the district. So, let's get started!

REFLECTION

What occurs to you when considering disproportionality? What questions do you have about your school? If you were the principal of the high school, what next steps would you be willing to take? If you were a teacher leader, to what action are you willing to commit? As you have followed Lupe throughout this book, what perspective is she bringing to the group? In what ways does this case story illustrate *institutionalizing cultural knowledge toward common outcomes for all students*?

_____

_____

_____

_____

Fittingly, one of the final case stories in this book is about graduation. Ms. Lopez, principal at the high school, and her counselors are busily reviewing data about who will and who may not graduate on time. Senior progress toward graduation is a yearlong concern that becomes amplified in the second semester.

HOW CLOSE ARE WE TO 100% GRADUATION?

Ms. Lopez has called a counselors' meeting to review the current senior class progress toward June graduation. Reviewing and assessing student progress toward graduation has been issued as a mandate by the district, a mandate that Ms. Lopez embraces enthusiastically. Each counselor has the responsibility for reviewing his or her current data. As they discuss student progress, counselors present their concerns at the meeting.

Head Counselor	*Ms. Lopez, I understand what you are trying to do here. I know we want every student to graduate on time. I heard what the superintendent said. But really? Really? When are we going to face the fact that it is just seems like an impossible goal. Some students are not going to graduate, and there is not much we can do about it. We can go over the numbers a hundred times; it is not going to change. 100% graduation is just not attainable, and stating it doesn't change it.*
Cynthia	*I have special education students, I have the EL students, and they just can't do it. They need more time. I don't know what to do. It doesn't seem fair to expect this from them.*
Freda	*I have done everything I can. I have referred them to adult school; I have referred them to continuation school, and community college. They just don't go. I have written the letters and just get angry phone calls in return. When are they going to learn to take responsibility?*
Edward	*It's 11 weeks before graduation. I do not know what we can do now.*
Cynthia	*When is someone going to talk about the elephant in the room? We have caseloads over 600; what do they expect us to do?*
Edward	*Don't forget about those other ones who are just so annoying . . . always asking always pestering about the same things. They take up so much of your time. You know the ones.*
Ms. Lopez	*Which ones?*
Edward	*The ones who won't take no for an answer. They just take up your time . . . and make you answer a million questions.*
Ms. Lopez	*Oh, the students who are on track to graduate ... score proficient and advanced . . . and really want to do well?*

Counselors are silent.

Ms. Lopez	*I agree that 100% graduation rate is an extraordinary goal. I would like you to consider this as we look at our students' data. How far along are some students? Let's look at where they are situated. About how many are on track?*

Counselors review data.

Ricardo	*From this, it appears 83% of our students are on track to graduate. All they have to do is pass the classes they are attending. There are now 6% that only need one or two make-up courses. We just need to make sure they finish them.*
Ms. Lopez	*So off the bat we have 89% of our senior class who are truly close to making June graduation. So what we can we do for them?*
Ricardo	*It appears 83% monitoring may be enough . . . but you know about senioritis . . .*
Ms. Lopez	*We should be deliberately monitoring and watching for signs of encouragement and agreement. It is it amazing that we have 89% so close to the finish line! We have to be aware of the tendency of students to let go and lose focus. We know this is a common phenomenon. Because they are on track does not mean we ignore them. It means we pay attention to them. So we monitor and watch, and look for signs, follow up to see they enroll . . .*
Freda	*Not just enroll . . . attend the tutoring sessions or class.*
Ms. Lopez	*However, let's talk about the 11% who may need more intensive or targeted services.*
Ricardo	*We need to target this group.*
Edward	*Well, but there are 4% that are clearly not going to make it, not in this time frame.*
Ms. Lopez	*So perhaps 100% graduation for this June may not be attainable, but is it conceivable that we could approach 100% graduation within 6 months? 12 months? 18 months? June graduation is our first goal, but our commitment does not end there. What can we do to ensure they do make it? How do we support the goal of completing their education and earning their diploma?*
Ricardo	*They need a plan—they need to know how they can complete the requirements.*
Freda	*We have to be clear; they do tend to get discouraged.*
Cynthia	*Hey, and don't discount them. I have had kids pull it off. Last year one of my seniors made up 42 credits.*

There are plenty of options. We need to make them aware of them.

Ricardo *So we need to prioritize the type of service and monitoring they need. Eighty-nine percent of students need monitoring support, 6% of the 11 targeted support, and 5% will need intensive support, with perhaps extra years on our site.*

Freda *But we also have to be smarter about our time management. I am going to say it rudely, . . . but . . . look when the students come here from other countries, they are great students and present challenges at the same time. We have to communicate clearly with them so they feel comfortable with their programs of study and decisions they have to make. We also need to be respectful and supportive, even intensively supportive in their courses.*

Ms. Lopez *So you are saying we need to target our efforts and time to support the students who need support. However, we must also learn to efficiently manage our conversations with all students. I am also hearing a need to clearly communicate to everyone what they need to do.*

Ricardo *So the goal is graduating, even past June.*

Ms. Lopez Yes. *The goal is 100% graduation rate, ultimately.*

The faculty meeting ended with everyone having a clearer, common focus on the outcomes for their students,

REFLECTION

What is emerging for you as you reflect on this case story? Who are you best represented by in the story? Why? What are some next steps by the principal? By the teachers?

GOING DEEPER

The Essential Element in this chapter is comprised of two very strong concepts—*institutionalizing* and *cultural knowledge*. Think about the dynamics of each of these concepts in combination with a commitment toward common outcomes for all students! As we have said earlier in this book, this commitment is the promise and the hope of the Common Core Standards. So, in what ways is your commitment to an equitable set of outcomes for all students supported by your school or district? How does your district and school support diverse learners to achieve high standards for college and career readiness? Use the space below to record your responses.

_____

_____

_____

_____

DIALOGIC ACTIVITY

With a group of your colleagues, continue to engage in a dialogue to reach shared understanding of a school culture *institutionalizing cultural knowledge by applying and connecting a commitment toward common outcomes for all students.* In what ways might a common commitment to the CCSS improve outcomes for all students? You are also invited to engage with colleagues in a brainstorming activity with advance caution to *avoid* trying to make decisions or to evaluate what is being offered as examples during the brainstorming event. What are the barriers to institutionalizing knowledge about the organizational culture of your school? What are the barriers to institutionalizing knowledge about the cultures of your students? In each case, what supports gaining knowledge about the culture of your school and the cultures of your school? Once the brainstorming activity has concluded, engage in dialogue about what might be some resources, strategies, and structures that could be developed, activated, and shared to support all learners, with an emphasis on *college and career readiness*?

_____

_____

_____

_____

FROM THINKING TO PLANNING TO ACTION

Chapters 7 through 11 presented the 5 Essential Elements integrated with standards for Quality Professional Learning in support of the Common

Core Standards. You have read and interacted with characters from case stories who are engaged in implementing phases of the professional learning plans to implement the Common core Standards. Now, you are ready to design your own plan of action. Chapter 12 provides you with a template and description for developing your Culturally Proficient Professional Learning Action Plan. It is time for you and your colleagues to move to action by making a commitment toward common outcomes for all students performing at different learning levels to prepare them for college and careers.

Part III

Move to Action

You are now well equipped with information and skills to Move to Action. The lone ingredient you, your colleagues, and your school need to provide is embodied in the timeless words Asa Hilliard used to title an article for *Educational Leadership* more than a decade ago:

Do we have the will to educate all children?

—Asa Hilliard, 1991, p. 31

The final section of this book invites and supports you and your colleagues to work with one another, with your communities, with your professional organizations, and whoever is appropriate in developing a template for moving forward. The six chapters that comprised Part I provided necessary building blocks for understanding equity and reform in ways that will empower you to consider the changes you will want to make in your educational practice and in your school or district. These six chapters deepened your learning and provided opportunities for personal reflection and dialogic experiences for exploring professional learning in community with colleagues.

The five chapters of Part II directed your learning in how to use the 5 Essential Elements as standards to guide your individual educational practice and to lead professional learning experiences with colleagues. Chapter 12 moves you to action! You have the opportunity and the invitation to design your and your school's Culturally Proficient Professional Learning Action Plan.

12 Ensuring a Culturally Proficient Professional Learning Plan

Common Core is not a set of controls to limit educators—it is a call to action. As a nation, we are stepping forward and proclaiming that we must do something differently on behalf of our children and our future.

—Cindy Marten, Superintendent
of San Diego Unified School District (2014)

GOING DEEPER

What is your reaction to Superintendent Marten's comments? What do the Common Core State Standards (CCSS) mean to you? What is your role in implementing and sustaining an environment in which educators can grow professionally and develop students who are prepared for college and career choices? What actions are you willing to take to step forward and proclaim to do something differently to serve educators and their students as a culturally proficient leader? Write your responses on the lines that follow.

_____

_____

_____

_____

This book provides an integration of the Essential Elements of Cultural Proficiency and the standards of professional learning. In Chapter 6, we presented our framework for understanding, and sustaining Culturally Proficient Professional Learning (Table 6.2) in support of the Common Core implementation. The framework displays the Essential Elements for Cultural Proficiency alongside the quality standards of professional learning. Also, in Chapter 6, we presented a rubric (Table 6.1) describing unproductive/productive and unhealthy/healthy behaviors grounded in the core values of culturally proficient educational practices (Tool 2: The Guiding Principles). In the absence of deeply held values inclusive of students' cultures, individuals and learning teams will experience difficulty in achieving the ultimate goal of narrowing and closing educational, access, and achievement gaps. Professional learning work is _the work of preparing and supporting educators to implement the Common Core Standards in ways that ensure all students are well prepared to make choices for college and careers._ Cultural Proficiency can be _the lens_ through which the educators view their work. Cultural Proficiency does not add a longer "to-do" list to our current work. Cultural Proficiency enhances and deepens that work, leading to high achievement for all students (Lindsey, Nuri Robins, & Terrell, 2009).

The purpose of this chapter is to provide you with the opportunity to deepen your thinking, expand your planning, and select your actions for using Cultural Proficiency as a lens to design, expand, and examine professional learning. This level of planning is to support you and your colleagues as you implement the Common Core Standards in ways that support all learners toward college and career readiness.

Professional development/learning has evolved during the past generation from isolated classrooms of teachers-as-independent-contractors attending occasional faculty information meetings and workshop-ways-of-learning to today's professional educators participating in formal structures of professional learning communities for sharing ideas, strategies, vision, practice, resources, and results. As teaching has shifted from a scope-and-sequence compliance model to a standards- and performance-based professional model, educators work collaboratively to design and develop grade- and school-level assessments, instructional strategies, and appropriate curriculum. These collaborative efforts are intentional and research-based (Hord & Sommers, 2008).

We offer one of Shirley Hord and William Sommers' key questions: "What should we intentionally learn in order to become more effective in our teaching so that students learn well?" (2008, p. 12). As you consider your personal action learning goals and the action learning goals for your school and district, what is ahead for you? We offer the following opportunities for you to deepen your thinking, your planning, and your actions.

DEEPEN YOUR THINKING ABOUT PROFESSIONAL LEARNING

Andy Hargreaves and Michael Fullan (2012) describe our profession of teaching as being at a new crossroads of education reform. One road can lead us to "getting tougher on teachers" (p. 45) while the other road can take us toward developing a profession that becomes "more inspiring, tough, and challenging, in itself" (p. 45). This second path they describe will come from collaborative leadership "that reconciles and integrates external accountability with personal and collective professional responsibility" (Fullan, 2012, p. 45). The reform and improvement in our profession will come from our recognizing our quality standards for professional learning as individuals and as teams. Looking back at Dilts and Bateson's nested levels for school improvement in Chapter 3, Table 3.4, investing in and improving teachers' capabilities through high-quality professional learning that honors and values students' cultures and communities will move us closer to improving their achievement.

Professional development and learning is one way to nurture the hearts, minds, and culture of the teaching profession. Too often, teacher evaluation processes focus on punitive and "fix-it" strategies. In this book, we offer ways to grow the profession organizationally and individually through the lens of Cultural Proficiency. This process may be a shift in thinking from deficient identification to asset building. Cultural Proficiency invites you to think of the professional learning standards as a set of guidelines for growth from where you are to becoming the teacher and leader you want to be. The remainder of this chapter guides you from your thinking to your planning to your action as a Culturally Proficient educator.

REFLECTION

In what ways has your thinking about professional learning shifted as you read this book? What new questions come to mind as you think of "growing" the profession? Of what are you most aware about your own professional learning needs and the Common Core State Standards? Take a few minutes and write about your own thinking at this point in your reading.

_____

_____

_____

_____

EXPAND YOUR PLANNING
ABOUT PROFESSIONAL LEARNING

Most schools experience no shortage of school plans. Plans are required for federal and state mandates that provide school funding. Regional accreditation organizations require school plans for memberships and ongoing accreditation. Schools and districts prepare elaborate plans for grant funds and are required to monitor that plan when funds are issued. Handbooks and workshops are provided for writing and maintaining schoolwide plans. Unfortunately, many of these plans are placed in elaborate binders, burned on CDs, displayed in prominent locations, and never consulted again until time for a future evaluation of how the school is using the resources.

The kind of planning we advocate for is consistent with the old adage _Plan your work and work your Plan._ We believe a thoughtful Culturally Proficient Professional Learning Action Plan (CPPLAP) will ensure equity through the Common Core State Standards. Transformative leaders take time to include and engage educators and community members in constructing a professional learning plan based on student needs and best and emerging educational practices. Once the plan is developed and made public, the implementation work begins. The plan is constantly monitored for gap analysis between what you wanted to accomplish and what you are actually achieving (gap analysis; Fisher, Frey, & Pumpian, 2012). Making the Professional Learning Action Plan public gives educators and community member's ownership of the goals and expectations as well as the action steps necessary to reach those goals. The components of the Culturally Proficient Professional Learning Action Plan include the following:

- **School Vision and Mission Statements**—The CPPLAP is aligned with your school's shared vision and mission. Community members who are charged with developing and writing the CPPLAP will review current alignment of vision and mission statements with who you say you are and who you demonstrate you are by your current actions.
- **Current Reality and Rationale**—Planners will identify the current needs based in reality by collecting and analyzing data to guide decisions about setting the outcomes and goals. Will the current professional learning strategies and structures meet the anticipated needs

of the Common Core Standards? What might be additional data that we collect to determine our needs, successes, and challenges?

- **Outcomes and Expectations**—The CPPLAP is designed to grow and support educators as you implement the Common Core Standards to ensure equity for students to be prepared to enter college and the workforce. Your planning team will determine what the outcomes and expectations are for your professional learning action steps. What will you accomplish as a result of the Culturally Proficient Professional Learning experiences, knowledge, and skills that will be developed in educators in your school? What is it you want educators to know and be able to do related to the Common Core so that all students can achieve at high levels?

- **Goals**—In order to reach the outcomes you have established for yourself and with your fellow educators, what goals must you establish? In what ways are these goals measurable and aligned with your vision and mission? We recommend the planners use SMART goals as you develop and write your CPPLAP. SMART goals are described as

Specific = Who, what, when, where, which, why?

Measurable = Concrete criteria for measuring success: How much, how many, how will we know?

Attainable = Develop knowledge, skills, attitudes, and resources to attain our goals: What do we need to be successful?

Realistic = Is our goal high enough, and are we willing to work hard enough to reach it?

Timely = Develop a specific time line for benchmarking. The goals must include both short- and long-term.

The goals need to be measurable so you and your team will benchmark (measure how you are doing at this point in time) your actions for points of success or *stuckness*. Benchmarking is a leadership action that helps the team move forward based on data rather than wonder how they are doing or assume the results are good or bad.

- **Culturally Proficient Action Steps**—The action steps are carefully planned behaviors based on best practices and assets-building approaches for Culturally Proficient educators. The planned actions are built on the 5 Essential Elements of Cultural Proficiency. Each of the elements enhances the professional learning environment and develops a school culture in support of all learners performing at levels higher than ever before. The action steps are the heart of the success of the CPPLAP.

- **Evaluation and Indicators of Success**—*So how will we know how we are doing?* That's the question you will ask as you and your team monitor your successes and challenges of implementing your professional learning plan. How will you measure success? How often will you measure your progress? What data will you collect? These are benchmarking questions to measure the progress of your actions. The results of analyzing these data are fed back into the plan in ways to support continuous learning. The plan itself may be revised as your team analyzes data that may improve educator's practice. Monitoring and supporting the plan is another way to sustain the learning communities toward common standards for all students.

Review Table 12.1 and think about questions you have as this table applies to your school and district. In what ways might this Action Plan template support your professional learning planning?

Table 12.1   Culturally Proficient Professional Learning Action Plan

Capital City High School
Our School Vision: **Our School Mission:**
Current Reality and Rationale: Assessment data (*and other information/observations*): What are our current professional learning plan and structures for support?
Outcomes: What is it we want to accomplish for our teachers and leaders? What is it we want educators to know and be able to do related to the Common Core so that all students can achieve at high levels?
Goal One (*use SMART criteria*): What goals will we need to establish to reach those outcomes? To what extent are these goals aligned with our vision/mission?   **Goal Two**   **Goal Three**

Capital City High School				
Culturally Proficient Action steps What actions will we take to reach our goals?	Person(s) responsible (*positions, not names*)	Resources: Materials and/or Personnel	Time line: When will we benchmark?	Funding:
Assessing cultural knowledge:				
Valuing diversity:				
Managing the dynamics of diversity:				
Adapting to diversity:				
Institutionalizing cultural knowledge:				

Evaluation and indicators of success *(toward achieving goal)*: How will we measure success? What will we use as benchmarks of success?

SMART Goals:

Specific = Who, what, when, where, which, why?

Measurable = Concrete criteria for measuring success: How much, how many, how will we know?

Attainable = Develop knowledge, skills, attitudes, and resources to attain our goals: What do we need to be successful?

Realistic = Is our goal high enough, and are we willing to work hard enough to reach it?

Timely, **T**angible = What is our sense of urgency? Can we see it and hear it and feel it and know when we have reached our goal/outcome?

REFLECTION

Take a few minutes and write your new thinking about the importance of developing an Action Plan. In what ways does this Action Plan template inform your work? How do the 5 Essential Elements enhance the Action Steps for the Professional Learning Plan?

SELECT YOUR ACTIONS IN A CULTURALLY PROFICIENT WAY

As you reflect on the content of this book, what comes to mind for you? The following questions intentionally use the personal pronoun "I" so you might use these questions to guide your thinking, planning, and actions:

Of what am I most intentional in my teaching and learning?

_____

_____

Who am I, in relation to my colleagues?

_____

_____

Who are we as a professional community?

_____

_____

What are we learning that will ensure equity through the Common Core Standards?

_____

_____

What are we doing with what we are learning about the Common Core?

_____

_____

Who else do we need to include in our community about implementing the Common Core, and how it relates to our professional learning?

_____

_____

What (additional) data would be helpful as we develop our Culturally Proficient Professional Learning Plan?

_____

_____

The final words of this book will be yours. Space is provided below for you to commit to actions steps. These final questions are designed to help you focus on your future actions and commitment to yourself and your learning community:

- In what ways am I willing to commit myself to use Cultural Proficiency as a lens through which I examine and design or redesign my current work focused on the Common Core?
- In what ways am I willing to commit my learning communities to use cultural proficiency as a lens through which we examine and design or redesign our current work focused on the Common Core?
- What are my short- and long-term goals? What will I/we accomplish with our commitment to this work?
- What are the first steps I will take? Second steps? What would my Personal Culturally Proficient Professional Learning Action Plan be?

Use this space to record your responses and your commitments:

_____

_____

_____

_____

_____

DIALOGIC ACTIVITY

The conversation continues as you and your colleagues engage in a dialogue to continue your shared understanding of a school culture *in support of all learners performing at levels higher than ever before.* In what ways does the Action Plan (CPPLAP) inform your implementation of the Common Core? What is currently in place in your school that supports implementation? Are you ready to write your Plan? Continue the dialogue throughout small learning communities in the school district. Once shared understanding has been reached, what step might you take to fully implement your Action Plan for professional learning in support of all learners, with emphasis on *college and career readiness*?

_____

_____

_____

_____

OUR INVITATION AND COMMITMENT TO YOU

We are partners with you in this journey toward culturally proficient educational practices. We invite you to engage with us about your experiences as you grow and develop in your profession. We'd like to hear your stories, your questions, and your commitments to this work. Please share your strategies, your learning, your actions, and your materials as you ensure equity through the implementation of the Common Core Standards. We look forward to conversation with you.

Contact us:

Delores is at dblindsey@aol.com

Karen is at kkearne@wested.org

Delia is at delia.estrada@lausd.net

Ray is at terrelr@muohio.edu

Randy is at randallblindsey@gmail.com

Resource A—Book Study Guide

A Culturally Proficient Response to the Common Core: Ensuring Equity Through Professional Learning

Delores B. Lindsey, Karen M. Kearney, Delia Estrada,
Raymond D. Terrell, & Randall B. Lindsey
Corwin, 2015

CHAPTER 1—COMMON CORE AND CULTURAL PROFICIENCY: A COMMITMENT TOWARD EQUITY

Content Questions to Consider

- In what ways do you describe equity?
- In what ways might educators and their students be "co-learners"?
- What do you understand the purpose of this book to be?

Personal Reaction Questions to Consider

- What is your reaction to the intent of this book?
- What is your reaction to examining and discussing equity, access, and achievement gaps in your school?

CHAPTER 2—HISTORY AND HOPE FOR CHANGING SCHOOLS

Content Questions to Consider

- How do you describe "mindfulness"?
- What are some examples of school reform in the last century?
- In what ways would you describe a history of equity and inequity?
- How do you describe transformative leadership?

Personal Reaction Question to Consider

- How might you either begin or deepen a consideration of equitable practices in your school or district?

CHAPTER 3—THE TOOLS OF CULTURAL PROFICIENCY

Content Questions to Consider

- Name the Tools of Cultural Proficiency.
- In what ways do you describe the *Inside-Out Process*?
- How do reflection and dialogue support the *Inside-Out Process*?
- Describe how and why culture is embraced as an asset to support Cultural Proficiency.
- In what ways are the Guiding Principles as core values consistent with how you view yourself and your school?
- Explain how the Guiding Principles serve to counter the Barriers to Cultural Proficiency.
- In what ways will the Essential Elements provide you with "action" steps on your journey toward Cultural Proficiency?

Personal Reaction Questions to Consider

- What is your reaction to the Barriers Section? To the Guiding Principles as core values?
  - Describe the manner in which the Essential Elements are informed and supported by the Guiding Principles.
  - In what ways do the Essential Elements serve as standards for personal, professional behavior?
- What is your reaction, personally or professionally, as you become acquainted with the Tools?
- What more do you want to know/learn about Cultural Proficiency?

CHAPTER 4—PROMISE OF THE COMMON CORE

Content Questions to Consider

- What do you understand the "promise" of the Common Core to be?
- In what ways do you describe the "shifts" taking place to support the Common Core?
- What challenges are ahead for implementation of the Common Core?
- What are some opportunities for students afforded by the Common Core?
- What are some opportunities for educators afforded by the Common Core?
- In what ways does "professional development" differ from "professional learning"?

Personal Reaction Questions to Consider

- What is your reaction to this chapter?
- To what extent does the "promise" of the Common Core resonate with you?
- What might be some opportunities ahead for your professional learning?

CHAPTER 5—LEADERSHIP AND THE COMMON CORE

Content Questions to Consider

- In what ways does the principal's role evolve when addressing the Common Core?
- In what key areas does leadership relate to student achievement?
- How might you describe shared leadership?
- In what ways does professional learning differ from professional development?

Personal Reaction Questions to Consider

- What is your reaction to this chapter?
- In what ways do you want to develop as leader?
- In what ways are values for social justice evident in your leadership style and behaviors?

CHAPTER 6—FROM STUCKNESS TO IMPLEMENTATION (OR FROM YIKES! TO YES!)

Content Questions to Consider

- How might you describe "stuckness"?
- In what ways might you illustrate collective efficacy and academic optimism?
- Describe the "why question" that is fundamental to the "inside-out" process of change.

Personal Reaction Questions to Consider

- How do you view your own professional learning horizon with regard to your school and the community within which it resides?
- How do you react to professional learning being a change force?
- In what ways might you reach out to others who seem to be stuck?

CHAPTER 7—ASSESSING CULTURAL KNOWLEDGE: COLLECTING, ANALYZING, AND USING DATA TO GUIDE DECISIONS

Content Questions to Consider

- In what ways do the Essential Elements serve as standards for professional learning?
- How might the Essential Elements be useful for you and your school?
- In what ways might studying data about student access and achievement inform *Assessing Cultural Knowledge*?
- In what ways do Lupe and her colleagues describe *Assessing Cultural Knowledge*?

Personal Reaction Questions to Consider

- In what ways is Cultural Proficiency a *journey*?
- How do you describe your understanding of *Assessing Cultural Knowledge*?
- In what ways can you and your school use the information from this chapter?

CHAPTER 8—VALUING DIVERSITY: DEVELOPING SKILLFUL LEADERS TO CREATE SUPPORT SYSTEMS FOR PROFESSIONAL LEARNING

Content Questions to Consider

- How might you describe the Essential Element, *Valuing Diversity*?
- In what ways do you describe support systems?
- What is the valuing diversity issue in the case story? Who needs help and why do you think it to be so?

Personal Reaction Questions to Consider

- What were your thoughts and personal reactions about the information in this chapter? In what ways do your reactions inform intentional use of support systems?
- In what ways might you and your school use the information from this chapter?

CHAPTER 9—MANAGING THE DYNAMICS OF DIVERSITY: CREATING AND SUSTAINING LEARNING COMMUNITIES

Content Questions to Consider

- How might you describe the Essential Element, *Managing the Dynamics of Diversity*?
- In what ways does managing the dynamics of difference help support learning communities to be vibrant?
- What is the dynamics of diversity issue in the case story? Who needs help and why do you think it to be so?

Personal Reaction Questions to Consider

- What were your thoughts and personal reactions about the information in this chapter?
- In what ways do your reactions inform your future choices for working in your school?
- In what ways can you and your school use the information from this chapter?

CHAPTER 10—ADAPTING TO DIVERSITY: APPLYING EVIDENCE-BASED APPROACHES TO ACTIVELY ENGAGE EDUCATORS IN IMPROVING PRACTICE

Content Questions to Consider

- Please describe the Essential Element, *Adapting to Diversity*.
- In what ways do evidence-based approaches align with adapting to the community one serves?
- What is the adapting to diversity issue in the case story? Who needs help and why do you think it to be so?

Personal Reaction Questions to Consider

- What were your thoughts and personal reactions about the information in this chapter? In what ways do your reactions inform your future choices for you and your school?
- In what ways can you and your school use the information from this chapter?

CHAPTER 11—INSTITUTIONALIZING CULTURAL KNOWLEDGE: APPLYING AND CONNECTING A COMMITMENT TOWARD COMMON OUTCOMES FOR ALL STUDENTS

Content Questions to Consider

- How do you describe the Essential Element, *Institutionalizing Cultural Knowledge*?
- You have been reading the phrase *"inside-out"* process throughout this book. What does it mean to you now? What has been added to your knowledge? In what ways does it apply to schools?
- In the context of this chapter, in what ways do you describe *transformative leadership*?
- What is the issue in the case story? Who needs help and why do you think it to be so?

Personal Reaction Questions to Consider

- What were your thoughts and personal reactions about the information in this chapter? In what ways do your reactions inform your future choices for you and your school?

- In what ways can you and your school use the information from this chapter?

CHAPTER 12—ENSURING A CULTURALLY PROFICIENT LEARNING PLAN

Content Questions to Consider

- In what ways do SMART goals support the work of Culturally Proficient Professional Learning?
- Why do conversations matter?

Personal Reaction Question to Consider

- What are your reactions in responding to the progression of prompts in this chapter?
- In what ways can you and your school use the information from this chapter?
- Now that you know what you know, what are you willing to do?

Resource B— Cultural Proficiency Books' Essential Questions

Book	Authors	Focus and Essential Questions
Cultural Proficiency: A Manual for School Leaders, 3rd ed., 2009	Randall B. Lindsey Kikanza Nuri Robins Raymond D. Terrell	This book is an introduction to cultural proficiency. The book provides readers with extended discussion of each of the tools and the historical framework for diversity work. • What is cultural proficiency? How does Cultural Proficiency differ from other responses to diversity? • In what ways do I incorporate the Tools of Cultural Proficiency into my practice? • How do I use the resources and activities to support professional development? • How do I identify barriers to student learning? • How do the guiding principles and essential elements support better education for students? • What does the "inside-out" process mean for me as an educator? • How do I foster challenging conversations with colleagues? • How do I extend my own learning?
Culturally Proficient Instruction: A Guide for People Who Teach, 3rd ed., 2012	Kikanza Nuri-Robins Randall B. Lindsey Delores B. Lindsey Raymond D. Terrell	This book focuses on the 5 Essential Elements and can be helpful to anyone in an instructional role. This book can be used as a workbook for a study group. • What does it mean to be a culturally proficient instructor? • How do I incorporate Cultural Proficiency into a school's learning community processes? • How do we move from "mindset" or "mental model" to a set of practices in our school? • How does my "cultural story" support being effective as an educator with my students? • In what ways might we apply the Maple View Story to our learning community?

(Continued)

(Continued)

Book	Authors	Focus and Essential Questions
		• In what ways can I integrate the guiding principles of cultural proficiency with my own values about learning and learners? • In what ways do the Essential Elements as standards inform and support our work with the Common Core Standards? • How do I foster challenging conversations with colleagues? • How do I extend my own learning?
The Culturally Proficient School: An Implementation Guide for School Leaders, 2nd ed., 2013	Randall B. Lindsey Laraine M. Roberts Franklin CampbellJones	This book guides the reader to examine their school as a cultural organization and to design and implement approaches to dialogue and inquiry. • In what ways do "Cultural Proficiency" and "school leadership" help me close achievement gaps? • What are the communication skills I need master to support my colleagues when focusing on achievement gap topics? • How do "transactional" and "transformational" changes differ and inform closing achievement gaps in my school/district? • How do I foster challenging conversations with colleagues? • How do I extend my own learning?
Culturally Proficient Coaching: Supporting Educators to Create Equitable Schools, 2007	Delores B. Lindsey Richard S. Martinez Randall B. Lindsey	This book aligns the Essential Elements with Costa and Garmston's Cognitive Coaching model. The book provides coaches, teachers, and administrators a personal guidebook with protocols and maps for conducting conversations that shift thinking in support of all students achieving at levels higher than ever before. • What are the coaching skills I need in working with diverse student populations?

Book	Authors	Focus and Essential Questions
		• In what ways do the Tools of Cultural Proficiency and Cognitive Coaching's States of Mind support my addressing achievement issues in my school? • How do I foster challenging conversations with colleagues? • How do I extend my own learning?
Culturally Proficient Inquiry: A Lens for Identifying and Examining Educational Gaps, 2008	Randall B. Lindsey Stephanie M. Graham R. Chris Westphal, Jr. Cynthia L. Jew	This book uses protocols for gathering and analyzing student achievement and access data. Rubrics for gathering and analyzing data about educator practices are also presented. A CD accompanies the book for easy downloading and use of the data protocols. • How do we move from the "will" to educate all children to actually developing our "skills" and doing so? • In what ways do we use the various forms of student achievement data to inform educator practice? • In what ways do we use access data (e.g., suspensions, absences, enrollment in special education or gifted classes) to inform schoolwide practices? • How do we use the four rubrics to inform educator professional development? • How do I foster challenging conversations with colleagues? • How do I extend my own learning?
Culturally Proficient Leadership: *The Personal Journey Begins Within,* **2009**	Raymond D. Terrell Randall B. Lindsey	This book guides the reader through the development of a cultural autobiography as a means to becoming an increasingly effective leader in our diverse society. The book is an effective tool for use by leadership teams. • How did I develop my attitudes about others' cultures? • When I engage in intentional cross-cultural communication, how can I use those experiences to heighten my effectiveness?

(Continued)

(Continued)

Book	Authors	Focus and Essential Questions
		• In what ways can I grow into being a culturally proficient leader? • How do I foster challenging conversations with colleagues? • How do I extend my own learning?
Culturally Proficient Learning Communities: Confronting Inequity Through Collaborative Curiosity, **2009**	Delores B. Lindsey Linda D. Jungwirth Jarvis V.N.C. Pahl Randall B. Lindsey	This book provides readers a lens through which to examine the purpose, the intentions, and the progress of learning communities to which they belong or wish to develop. School and district leaders are provided protocols, activities, and rubrics to engage in actions focused on the intersection of race, ethnicity, gender, social class, sexual orientation and identity, faith, and ableness with the disparities in student achievement. • What is necessary for a learning community to become a "culturally proficient learning community?" • What is organizational culture and how do I describe my school's culture in support of equity and access? • What are "curiosity" and "collaborative curiosity," and how do I foster them at my school/district? • How will "breakthrough questions" enhance my work as a learning community member and leader? • How do I foster challenging conversations with colleagues? • How do I extend my own learning?
The Cultural Proficiency Journey: Moving Beyond Ethical Barriers Toward Profound School Change, **2010**	Franklin CampbellJones Brenda CampbellJones Randall B. Lindsey	This book explores cultural proficiency as an ethical construct. It makes transparent the connection between values, assumptions, and beliefs, and observable behavior, making change possible and sustainable. The book is appropriate for book study teams. • In what ways does "moral consciousness" inform and support my role as an educator?

Book	Authors	Focus and Essential Questions
		• How does a school's "core values" become reflected in assumptions held about students? • What steps do I take to ensure that my school and I understand any low expectations we might have? • How do we recognize that our low expectations serve as ethical barriers? • How do I foster challenging conversations with colleagues? • How do I extend my own learning?
Culturally Proficient Education: An Assets-based Response to Conditions of Poverty, **2010**	Randall B. Lindsey Michelle S. Karns Keith Myatt	This book is written for educators to learn how to identify and develop the strengths of students from low-income backgrounds. It is an effective learning community resource to promote reflection and dialogue. • What are "assets" that students bring to school? • How do we operate from an "assets-based" perspective? • What are my and my school's expectations about students from low-income and impoverished backgrounds? • How do I foster challenging conversations with colleagues? • How do I extend my own learning?
Culturally Proficient Collaboration: Use and Misuse of School Counselors, **2011**	Diana L. Stephens Randall B. Lindsey	This book uses the lens of Cultural Proficiency to frame the American Association of School Counselor's performance standards and the Education Trust's Transforming School Counseling Initiative as means for addressing issues of access and equity in schools in collaborative school leadership teams. • How do counselors fit into achievement-related conversations with administrators and teachers? • What is the "new role" for counselors? • How does this "new role" differ from existing views of school counselor?

(Continued)

(Continued)

Book	Authors	Focus and Essential Questions
		• What is the role of site administrators in this new role of school counselor? • How do I foster challenging conversations with colleagues? • How do I extend my own learning?
A Culturally Proficient Society Begins in School: Leadership for Equity, **2011**	Carmella S. Franco Maria G. Ott Darline P. Robles	This book frames the life stories of three superintendents through the lens of Cultural Proficiency. The reader is provided the opportunity to design or modify his or her own leadership for equity plan. • In what ways is the role of school superintendent related to equity issues? • Why is this topic important to me as a superintendent or aspiring superintendent? • What are the leadership characteristics of a Culturally Proficient school superintendent? • How do I foster challenging conversations with colleagues? • How do I extend my own learning?
The Best of Corwin: Equity, **2012**	Randall B. Lindsey, Ed.	This edited book provides a range of perspectives of published chapters from prominent authors on topics of equity, access, and diversity. It is designed for use by school study groups. • In what ways do these readings support our professional learning? • How might I use these readings to engage others in learning conversations to support all students learning and all educators educating all students?
Culturally Proficient Practice: Supporting Educators of English Learning Students Learners, **2012**	Reyes L. Quezada Delores B. Lindsey Randall B. Lindsey	This book guides readers to apply the 5 Essential Elements of Cultural Competence to their individual practice and their school's approaches to equity. The book works well for school study groups. • In what ways do I foster support for the education of English learning students? • How can I use action research strategies to inform my practice with English learning students?

Book	Authors	Focus and Essential Questions
		• In what ways might this book support all educators in our district/school? • How do I foster challenging conversations with colleagues? • How do I extend my own learning?
A Culturally Proficient Response to LGBT Communities: A Guide for Educators, 2013	Randall B. Lindsey Richard Diaz Kikanza Nuri-Robins Raymond D. Terrell Delores B. Lindsey	This book guides the reader to understand sexual orientation in a way that provides for the educational needs of all students. The reader explores values, behaviors, policies, and practices that impact lesbian, gay, bisexual and transgender (LGBT) students, educators, and parents/guardians. • How do I foster support for LGBT colleagues, students, and parents/guardians? • In what ways does our school represent a value for LGBT members? • How can I create a safe environment for all students to learn? • To what extent is my school an environment where it is safe for the adults to be open about their sexual orientation? • How do I reconcile my attitudes toward religion and sexuality with my responsibilities as a PreK–12 educator? • How do I foster challenging conversations with colleagues? • How do I extend my own learning?
A Culturally Proficient Response to the Common Core: Ensuring Equity Through Professional Learning, 2015	Delores B. Lindsey Karen M. Kearney Delia Estrada Raymond D. Terrell Randall B. Lindsey	This book guides the reader to view and use the Common Core State Standards as a vehicle for ensuring all demographic groups of students are fully prepared for college and careers. • In what ways do I use this book to deepen my learning about equity? • In what ways do I use this book to deepen my learning about CCSS? • In what ways do I use this book with colleagues to deepen our work on equity and on the CCSS? • How can I and we use the Action Planning guide as an overlay for our current school planning?

References

Almy, Sarah. (2012, March). *Instructional supports—The missing piece in stated education standards.* Oakland, CA: Education Trust.

Archibald, Sarah. (2011). *High-quality professional development for all teachers: Effectively allocating resources.* Washington, DC: National Comprehensive Center for Teacher Quality. Retrieved from http://www.gtlcenter.org/sites/default/files/ docs/HighQualityProfessionalDevelopment.pdf

Armstrong, David A., Henson, Kenneth T., & Savage, Tom V. (2005). *Teaching today: An introduction to education* (7th ed.). Upper Saddle River, NJ: Pearson.

Baldoni, John. (2013, December 22nd). SmartBlog on Leadership. Retrieved from http://smartblogs.com/leadership/2013/12/22/take-a-hard-look-in-the-mirror

Banks, James A. (2006). *Race, culture and education: The selected works of James A. Banks.* New York, NY: Routledge.

Beatty, Barbara. (2012). Rethinking compensatory education: Historical perspectives on race, class, culture, language, and the discourse of the "disadvantaged child." *Teachers College Record, 114*(6), 1–11.

Berry, Barnett, Daughtrey, Alesha, & Wieder, Alan. (2009). *Closing the achievement gap.* Carrborro, NC: Center for Teaching Quality.

Borrero, Noah E., Yeh, Christine J., Crivir, I. Cruz, & Suda, Jolene F. (2012). Schools as context for "othering" youth and promoting cultural assets. *Teachers College Record, 114*(2), 1–37.

Brennan, Celina. (2014, February 19). *Personalized professional development elements: Supporting the CCSS transition.* The Whole Child Blog. Retrieved from http://www.wholechildeducation.org/blog/personalized-professional-development-elements-supporting-the-ccss

California Department of Education. (2013, December). *The superintendent's quality professional learning standards.* Sacramento, CA: California Department of Education, Professional Learning Support Division.

California Department of Education & the Commission on Teacher Credentialing. (2012, September). *Greatness by design: Supporting outstanding teaching to sustain a golden state.* Sacramento, CA: Authors.

Canole, Mary, & Young, Michelle. (2013, June). *Standards for educational leaders: An analysis.* Washington, DC: Council of Chief State School Officers (CCSSO). Retrieved from http://www.ccsso.org/Resources/Publications/Standards_for_Educational_Leaders_An Analysis.html

Clark, Constance, & Cookson, Peter. (2012, November). *High standards help struggling students: New evidence.* Washington, DC: Education Sector.

Clifford, Matthew, & Mason, Christine. (2013, November). *Leadership for the Common Core: More than one thousand school principals respond.* Reston, VA: National Association of Elementary School Principals.

Coggshall, Jane. (2012). *Toward the effective teaching of new college- and career-ready standards: Making professional learning systemic* (A Research-to-Practice Brief). Washington, DC: Center on Great Teachers and Leaders. Retrieved from http://www.tqsource.org/publications/TowardEffectiveTeaching.pdf

Common Core State Standards (CCSS). (2014). Available at http://www.core standards.org/

Common Core State Standards for English Language Arts & Literacy in History/ Social Studies, Science, and Technical Subjects. (2014). Available at http:// www.corestandards.org/ELA-Literacy/

Common Core State Standards for Mathematics. (2014). Available at http://www .corestandards.org/Math/

Council of Chief State School Officers (2008). *Educational leadership policy standards: ISLLC 2008 as adopted by the national policy board for education administration.* Washington, DC: Author.

Cross, Terry (1989). *Toward a culturally competent system of care.* Washington, DC: Georgetown University Child Development Program, Child and Adolescent Service System Program.

Darling-Hammond, Linda. (2007). The flat earth and education: How America's commitment to equity will determine our future. *Educational Researcher, 36,* 318–334.

Darling-Hammond, Linda. (2012). *Creating a comprehensive system for evaluating and supporting effective teaching.* Stanford, CA: Stanford Center for Opportunity Policy in Education.

Deal, Terrence, & Kennedy, Allan. (1982). *Corporate cultures: Understanding rites and rituals in corporate culture.* Harmondsworth, UK: Penguin.

Delpit, Lisa. (1995). *Other people's children: Cultural conflicts in the classroom.* New York, NY: New Press.

DeWitt, Peter. (2013, December 23). Today's guest post is Jenni Donohoo. Retrieved from http://blogs.edweek.org/edweek/finding_common_ground/2013/12/ fostering_teacherleadership_through_collaborative_inquiry.html

Dilts, Robert. (1990). *Changing belief systems with NLP.* Capitola, CA: Meta.

Dilts, Robert. (1994). *Effective presentation skills.* Capitola, CA: Meta.

Dove, Maria G., & Honigsfeld, Andrea. (2013). *Common Core for the not-so-common-learner: English language arts series, grades K-5.* Thousand Oaks, CA: Corwin.

Easton, Lois. (2008). From professional development to professional learning. *Phi Delta Kappan, 89,* 755–759.

Education First and Achieve. (2012, March). *A strong state role in common core state standards implementation: Rubric and self-assessment tool* (Draft). Washington, DC: Author.

Education Trust-West. (2012). *Catching up to the Core: Common sense strategies for accelerating access to the Common Core in California.* Oakland, CA. Author.

Elmore, Richard. (2000). *Building a new structure for leadership.* Washington, DC: The Albert Shanker Institute.

Farbman, David, Goldberg, David, & Miller, Tiffany. (2014, January). *Redesigning and expanding school time to support Common Core implementation.* Washington, DC: Center for American Progress.

Fisher, Douglas, Frey, Nancy, & Pumpian, Ian. (2012). *How to create a culture of achievement in your school and classroom.* Alexandria, VA: Association of Supervision and Curriculum Development.

Fixsen, Dean, & Blase, Karen. (2009). Implementation: The missing link between research and practice. *NIRN Implementation Brief, 1.*

Fixen, Dean, Blase, Karen, Horner, Bob, Sims, Barbar, & Sugai, George. (2013, September). *Scaling-up brief* (No. 3). Chapel Hill: University of North Carolina, FPG Child Development Center. Retrieved from http://sisep.fpg.unc.edu/sites/sisep.fpg.unc.edu/files/resources/SISEP-Brief1-Scalingup-01-2014.pdf

Freire, Paulo. (1998). *Pedagogy of hope: Reliving pedagogy of the oppressed.* New York, NY: Continuum.

Fullan, Michael. (2003). *The moral imperative of school leadership.* Thousand Oaks, CA: Corwin.

Fullan, Michael. (2011). *Change leader: Learning to do what matters most.* San Francisco, CA: Jossey-Bass.

Garmston, Robert J., & Wellman, Bruce M. (1999). *The adaptive school: A sourcebook for developing collaborative groups.* Norwood, MA: Christopher-Gordon.

Garmston, Robert J., & Wellman, Bruce M. (2013). *The presenter's fieldbook: A practical guide.* New York, NY: Roman & Littlefield.

Gay, Geneva. (2000). *Culturally responsive teaching: Theory, research and practice.* New York, NY: Teachers College Press.

Gewertz, Catherine. (2014, March 5). Studies follow four districts moving toward common core. *Education Week*, p. 12.

Gjaja, Marin, Puckett, J., & Ryder, Matt. (2014, February 19). When it comes to school funding, equity is the key. *Education Week*, pp. 30–31.

Gleason, Sonia Caus, & Gerzon, Nancy. (2013). *Growing into equity: Professional learning and personalization in high-achieving schools.* Thousand Oaks, CA: Corwin.

Gregory, Anne, Bell, James, & Pollock, Mica. (2014, March). *How educators can eradicate disparities in school discipline: A briefing paper on school-based interventions.* Bloomington, IN: The Equity Project at Indiana University, Center for Evaluation and Education Policy.

Hamilton, Leah, & Mackinnon, Anne. (2013). *Carnegie challenge—Opportunity by design: New high school models for student success.* New York, NY: Carnegie Corporation. Retrieved from http://carnegie.org/programs/urban-and-higher-education/new-designs-innovation-in-classroom-school-college-and-system-design/opportunity-by-design-new-high-school-models-for-student-success/

Hargreaves, Andy, & Fullan, Michael. (2012). *Professional capital: Transforming teaching in every school.* New York, NY: Teachers College Press.

Herold, Benjamin, & Molnar, Michele. (2014, March 5). Research questions common-core claims by publishers. *Education Week*, p. 1.

Hilliard, Asa. (1991). *Do we have the will to educate all children? Educational Leadership, 40*(1), 31–36.

Honig, Meredith, Copland, Michael, Rainey, Lidia, Lorton, Juli Anna, & Newton, Morena. (2010). *Central office transformation for district-wide teaching and learning improvement.* Seattle, WA: Center for the Study of Teaching and Policy, University of Washington.

Hord, Shirley M., & Roy, Patricia. (2014). Creating learning communities. In Ann Lieberman, Lynne Miller, Patricia Roy, Shirley M. Hord, & Valerie Von Frank (Eds.), *Reach the highest standard in professional learning: Learning communities (pp. 19–60).* Thousand Oaks, CA: Corwin.

Hord, Shirley M., & Sommers, William L. (2008). *Leading professional learning communities: Voices from research and practice.* Thousand Oaks, CA: Corwin.

Hoy, Wayne K., Tarter, C. John, & Woolfolk Hoy, Anita. (2006). Academic optimism of schools: A force for student achievement. *American Educational Research Journal, 43,* 425–446.

Hulce, Carla, Hoehn, Natasha, O'Day, Jennifer, & Walcott, Catherine. (2013, February). *California and the common core state standards: Early steps, early opportunities.* Washington, DC: American Institute for Research.

Hutt, Ethan. (2012). Formalism over function: Compulsion, courts, and the rise of educational formalism in America, 1870–1930. *Teachers College Record, 114*(1), 1–27.

Johnson, Susan Moore, Kraft, Matthew, & Papay, John. (2012). How context matters in high-need schools: The effects of teachers' working conditions on their professional satisfaction and their students' achievement. *Teachers College Record, 114*(10), 1–39.

Ladson-Billings, Gloria. (1994). *The dreamkeepers: Successful teachers of African American children.* San Francisco, CA: Jossey-Bass.

Learning Forward. (2011). *Standards for professional learning.* Oxford, OH: Author. Retrieved from http://learningforward.org/standards-for-professional-learning

Leithwood, Kenneth, Louis, Karen Seashore, Anderson, Stephen, & Wahlstrom, Kayla. (2004). *How leadership influences student learning.* New York, NY: The Wallace Foundation. Retrieved from http://www. wallacefoundation.org/knowledge-center/school-leadership/key-research/Documents/How-Leadership-Influences-Student-Learning.pdf

Lemov, Doug. (2013, May). *From "professional development" to "practice": Getting better at getting better.* Milwaukee, WI: Wisconsin Policy Research Institute.

Leo, Sheri, & Coggshall, Jane. (2013, September). *Creating coherence—Common Core State Standards, teacher evaluation, and professional learning.* Washington, DC: American Institutes for Research.

Lhamon, Catherine. (2014, March 21). *Five new facts from the Civil Rights Data Collection.* HomeRoom: The Official Blog of the U.S. Department of Education. Retrieved from http://www.ed.gov/blog/2014/03/five-new-facts-from-the-civil-rights-data-collection/

Lieberman, Ann, & Miller, Lynne. (2014). Unpacking professional learning communities. In Ann Lieberman, Lynne Miller, Patricia Roy, Shirley M. Hord, & Valerie Von Frank (Eds.), *Reach the highest standard in professional learning: Learning communities (pp. 1–18).* Thousand Oaks, CA: Corwin & Learning Forward.

Lindsey, Delores B., Martinez, Richard S., & Lindsey, Randall B. (2007). *Culturally proficient coaching: Supporting educators to create equitable schools.* Thousand Oaks, CA: Corwin.

Lindsey, Delores B., Terrell, Raymond D., Nuri, Kikanza J., & Lindsey, Randall B. (2007, May/June). Focus on assets, overcome barriers. *Leadership, 39*(5), 12–15.

Lindsey, Randall B., Diaz, Richard, M., Nuri-Robins, Kikanza, Terrell, Raymond D., & Lindsey, Delores B. (2013). *A culturally proficient response to LGBT communities: A guide for educators.* Thousand Oaks, CA: Corwin.

Lindsey, Randall B., Graham, Stephanie, M., Westphal, R. Chris, Jr., & Jew, Cynthia L. (2008). *Culturally proficient inquiry: A lens for identifying and examining educational gaps.* Thousand Oaks, CA: Corwin.

Lindsey, Randall B., Karns, Michelle S., & Myatt, Keith. (2010). *Culturally proficient education: An asset-based approach to conditions of poverty.* Thousand Oaks, CA: Corwin.

Lindsey, Randall B., Nuri Robins, Kikanza, & Terrell, Raymond D. (2009). *Cultural proficiency: A manual for school leaders* (3rd ed.). Thousand Oaks, CA: Corwin.

Lindsey, Randall B., Roberts, Laraine M., & CampbellJones, Franklin. (2013). *The culturally proficient school: An implementation guide for school leaders* (2nd ed.). Thousand Oaks, CA: Corwin.

Los Angeles Times Editorial Board Common Core learning curve. (2014, March 14). Retrieved from http://www.latimes.com/opinion/editorials/la-ed-common-core-two-20140314,0,919887.story#ixzz2wYZetsU7

Louis, Karen Seashore, Leithwood, Kenneth, Wahlstrom, Kayla, & Anderson, Stephen. (2010). *Investigating the links to improved student learning: Final report of research findings. Learning from leadership Project.* Minneapolis: CAREI, University of Minnesota.

Marten, Cindy. (2014, March 23). New goals focus of Authentic Learning. *The Union Tribune*, pp. SD5–SD7.

McGuigan, Leigh, & Hoy, Wayne K. (2006, September). Principal leadership: Creating a culture of academic optimism to improve achievement for all students, leadership and policy in schools. *Leadership and Policy in Schools, 5*, 203–229.

Meier, Deborah. (2002). *In schools we trust: Creating real learning communities in an era of testing and bureaucracy.* Boston, MA: Beacon Press.

National Assessment of Educational Progress. (2007). *The nation's report card.* Available from http://nces.ed.gov/nationsreportcard/pubs/main2007/2007494.asp

Nieto, Sonia, & Bode, Patty. (2012). *Affirming diversity: The sociopolitical context of multicultural education* (6th ed.). Boston, MA: Pearson.

No Child Left Behind Act of 2001 (NCLB), Pub. L. No. 107–110, 115 Stat. 1425 (2002).

Nuri-Robins, Kikanza, Lindsey, Delores B., Lindsey, Randall B., & Terrell, Raymond D. (2012). *Culturally proficient instruction: A guide for people who teach* (3rd ed.). Thousand Oaks, CA: Corwin.

Pappano, Laura. (2010). *Inside school turnarounds: Urgent hopes, unfolding stories.* Cambridge, MA: Harvard Education Press.

Polis, Jared, & Gibson, Chris. (2014, February 19). Broadband access is critical. *Education Week*, p. 30.

Quezada, Reyes L., Lindsey, Delores B., & Lindsey, Randall B. (2012). *Culturally Proficient Practice: Supporting Educators of English Learning Students.* Thousand Oaks, CA: Corwin.

Rebora, Anthony. (2013, March 13). Charlotte Danielson on teaching and the Common Core, *Education Week: Teacher.*

The Regional Equity Assistance Centers. (2013). *How the Common Core must ensure equity by fully preparing every student for postsecondary success: Recommendations from the Regional Equity Assistance Centers on implementation of the Common Core State Standards.* San Francisco, CA: WestEd.

Rothman, Robert. (2013, August). *Common core state standards 101.* Washington, DC: Alliance for Excellent Education.

Sanders, Nancy, & Kearney, Karen. (2008). *Performance expectations and indicators—An ISLLC guide to implementing leaders' standards and a companion guide to the Educational Leadership Policy Standards: ISLLC 2008.* Washington, DC: Council of Chief State School Officers.

Schein, Edgar H. (2010). *Organizational culture and leadership* (4th ed.). San Francisco, CA: Jossey-Bass.

Senge, Peter, Cambron-McCabe, Nelda, Lucas, Timothy, Smith, Bryan, Dutton, James, & Kleiner, Art. (2000). *Schools that learn: A fifth discipline fieldbook for educators, parents, and everyone who cares about education.* New York, NY: Doubleday.

Shields, Carolyn M. (2010). Transformative leadership: Working for equity in diverse contexts. *Educational Administration Quarterly, 46,* 558–589.

Sinek, Simon. (2009). *Start with why: How great leaders inspire everyone to take action.* New York, NY: Portfolio, Penguin Group.

Smith, Mark K. (1996/2000). *Curriculum theory and practice* [Webpage]. Retrieved from www.infed.org/biblio/b-curric.htm.

Smith, Page A., & Hoy, Wayne K. (2007). Academic optimism and student achievement in urban elementary schools. *Journal of Educational Administration, 45,* 556–568.

Span, Christopher, & Rivers, Ishwanzya, D. (2012). Reassessing the achievement gap: An intergenerational comparison of African American student achievement before and after compensatory education and the Elementary and Secondary Education Act. *Teachers College Record, 114*(6), 1–17.

Spencer, John. (2013). *Equality in education law and policy, 1954–2010.* New York, NY: Cambridge University Press.

Strauss, Valerie. (2013, May 3). "We're number umpteenth!": The myth of lagging schools. Article by Alfie Kohn. Retrieved from http://www.washingtonpost.com/blogs/answer-sheet/wp/2013/05/3

Superfine, Benjamin Michael. (2013). *Equality in education law and policy, 1954–2010.* Cambridge, MA: Cambridge University Press.

Theoharis, George. (2007). Social justice educational leaders and resistance: Toward a theory of social justice leadership. *Educational Administration Quarterly, 43,* 221–258.

U.S. Department of Education. (2010, March). *A blueprint for reform: The reauthorization of the Elementary and Secondary Education Act.* Retrieved from http://www2.ed.gov/policy/elsec/leg/blueprint/

Vega, Andrew. (2013, September 19). Don't fear the Common Core. *Los Angeles Times,* pp. A17.

Voltz, Deborah H., Sims, Michele Jean, & Nelson, Betty. (2010). *Connecting teachers, students, and standards: Strategies for success in diverse and inclusive classrooms.* Alexandria, VA: ASCD.

Wagner, Tony, Kegan, Robert, Lahey, Lisa, Lemons, Richard W., Garnier, Jude, Helsing, Deborah, . . . Rasmussen, Harriette Thurber. (2006). *Change leadership: A practical guide to transforming our schools.* San Francisco, CA: Jossey-Bass.

The Wallace Foundation. (2013, January). *The school principal as leader: Guiding schools to better teaching and learning.* New York, NY: Author.

Wei, Ruth Chung, Darling-Hammond, Linda, Andree, Alethea, Richardson, Nicole, & Orphanos, Stelios. (2009). *Professional learning in the learning profession: A status report on teacher development in the U.S. and abroad.* Dallas, TX: National Staff Development Council. Retrieved from http://www.arts.unco.edu/ciae/institute/2012%20Resources/2012%20Jumpdrive%20 Resources/Mark%20Hudson/nsdc_profdev_tech_report.pdf

Weick, Karl E. (1979). *The social psychology of organizing* (2nd ed.). New York, NY: McGraw Hill.

Williams, Trish, Kirst, Michael, & Haertel, Edward. (2010). *Gaining ground in the middle grades: Why some schools do better.* Mountain View, CA: EdSource.

Wilmore, Elaine L. (2002). *Principal leadership: Applying the new Educational Leadership Constituent Council (ELCC) standards,* Thousand Oaks, CA: Corwin.

Zacarian, Debbie. (2013). *Mastering academic language: A framework for supporting student achievement.* Thousand Oaks, CA: Corwin.

Index

A SAGE Company

Corwin is committed to improving education for all learners by publishing books and other professional development resources for those serving the field of PreK–12 education. By providing practical, hands-on materials, Corwin continues to carry out the promise of its motto: **"Helping Educators Do Their Work Better."**